Dancing from the Inside Out

UD WOMEN'S CENTER

Dancing from the Inside Out

GRACE-FILLED REFLECTIONS ON GETTING OLDER

Westina Matthews

CHURCH
PUBLISHING
INCORPORATED

Church Publishing
19 East 34th Street
New York, NY 10016
www.churchpublishing.org

Cover design by Marc Whitaker, MTWdesign
Typeset by PerfecType, Nashville, Tennessee

A record of this book is available from the Library of Congress.

ISBN-13: 978-1-64065-158-6 (pbk.)
ISBN-13: 978-1-64065-159-3 (ebook)

To my Great Aunt, Betsy G. Berry (1919–2019)
who taught me how to dance from the inside out

CONTENTS

DANCING FROM THE
INSIDE OUT

Tonight, I danced to Luther, Aretha, Isaac, and Maxwell. I was on the dance floor, joining others in the electric slide. Alone, and yet with others. Borrowing husbands and grabbing girlfriends. Dancing, dancing, dancing.

Oh, the joy of being over 50 is that I dance now from the inside out. No longer moving from the outside in . . . no longer to every beat . . . but rather, dancing to the beat I have within. Every other beat. Every three beats. Moving slow, but moving.

Just dancing . . . dancing . . . dancing. Popping fingers softly, swaying hips slightly, feet moving to the beat of the rhythm of my joy.

Not worrying about tomorrow. Not remembering yesterday. Just out on the dance floor, moving to the beat, eyes closed, head back, moving slowly, feeling the wonderful energy of me being ME in the moment. Smiling, laughing, enjoying being ME.

In the moment . . . I'm happy. In the moment . . . I'm free.

All I want to do right now is dance. Feel the music pulsating in me. Twirling around, standing my ground. Laughing with glee. Dancing from the inside out.

Portions of this essay first appeared as "I Need to Dance More, Alleluia!," in *Wisdom Found: Stories of Women Transfigured By Faith* (Cincinnati, OH: Forward Movement, 2011). Used with permission.

INTRODUCTION

I have kept a journal for almost fifty years in sporadic fits and starts. I am much better at being faithful to my journaling during the good times. Come the hard choices and the difficult times in life—I leave only blank pages behind. Except for my reflections. Often, I pick up the pen or head to the computer or thumb my way through the Notes app on my cell phone. *Dancing from the Inside Out: Grace-Filled Reflections on Growing Older* is a compilation of many of these reflections written over the years.

I have worked since I was ten years old. My first job was as a newspaper girl, delivering the weekly local paper every Wednesday afternoon to fifty anxiously awaiting residents in our small village in Yellow Springs, Ohio. One Saturday morning when I was about twelve years old, my father woke me up and told me that we were going to go get a Social Security card (this is long before the days of receiving one at birth). I asked my Dad why, to which he answered, "Because you are going to work." End of story.

And work I have done for the past sixty years, with little hiatus. I have always had jobs: babysitting, shelving books at the library, resident assistant in the dorm, receptionist at the candy counter, teacher, secretary, grant maker, banker, program officer, professor. Not working was never an option. I was going to work. I had to work. It makes me think that my father (who was an African Methodist Episcopal minister) must have read Chaung Tzu, a fourth-century BCE Chinese Taoist teacher

---

Portions of this introduction first appeared as "Spirituality in the Workplace," in *Finding God Day By Day* (Cincinnati, OH: Forward Movement, 2010). Used with permission.

who wrote, "Produce! Get results! Make money! Make friends! Make changes! Or you will die in despair!"

As I "prepared to prepare" for my retirement, I studied to become a spiritual director and retreat leader, an inspirational speaker, an author of contemplative books and essays, and an adjunct professor at a seminary. I embraced leaving the corporate world after twenty-four years with unexpected enthusiasm and expectation. I was not sure what I would be doing, but I certainly knew what I would *not* be doing: withering away in despair. And I was going to begin dancing from the inside out!

As convinced as I was that something good was about to unfold, nothing prepared me for the transition—and transformation—from wearing St. John suits, having an administrative assistant, and flying business class, to a life of carrying a backpack, wearing blue jeans, sitting in Harvard Yard thanks to a fellowship, working at the Jackie Robinson Foundation, and then relocating to an island in the South where I could ride my bicycle most days. Leaving New York City after almost thirty years has provided me with an unexpected gift . . . the gift of time. And with large parts of the day now spent in solitude, I finally am able to begin to listen to that still quiet voice within me and engage in discerning my own grace-filled embracing of getting older.

In *Soul at Work*, Margaret Benefiel suggests that the discernment process requires the ability to "listen to where God might be speaking . . . ; patience in waiting for God's answer; an ability to live with ambiguity; and a willingness to test the discernment by its fruits."*

The process of redefining who one is and who one is becoming is a lifelong process, and often not an easy one. Richard Rohr, in his Daily Meditations (December 29, 2014), reminds us that "The task of searching out and embracing shadow—the parts of yourself that you hide or ignore—is ongoing, the work of a lifetime. Let the people and circumstances that 'push your buttons' be your teachers. Look for yourself with a loving gaze in the mirror of both your enemies and those who enthrall you." How does one know if one is answering God's call or whether God

---

*Margaret Benefiel, *Soul at Work: Spiritual Leadership in Organizations* (New York: Seabury Books, 2005), 54.

is answering one's prayers? Is there life after retirement? Can one find a new beginning? What's next?

As the seasons unfolded over these past years, my life has continued to be filled with new insights; and I continue to yearn to have a better understanding of me and who I am becoming as I grow older. Through these reflections, I invite you to join me as I learn simply to "live into the questions" and to dance from the inside out.

1

Dancing to
Every Other Beat

Getting from Here to There

I t was my sister on the phone. "I'm lost."

My friends and I looked at one another wondering what to do next (this was before texting, GPS, and Siri). She had driven upstate to meet me in a city where I was visiting. No one in the house was from the area, so we were essentially of no help. Finally, Kathy came up with a great idea.

"Tell her to drive around until she gets to someplace where we know where she is, and then call us back."

We all laughed hysterically, more at our own predicament than my sister's. Eventually, we were finally able to figure out where she was, and someone volunteered to hop in their car and lead her back.

I thought about that story while visiting a dear friend recently. While she began preparing lunch in her kitchen, I slid on a stool at the counter. Elbows propped on counter, chin resting in hands, I eagerly awaited not only for the meal but also for whatever else would be served up in conversation.

"The other day, someone told me, 'You know in another three years, you will be eighty.' Now what do you suppose she meant by that?" my friend asked with raised eyebrow. "And what am I to do with this information, where do I go from here?" she pondered, clearly perplexed.

Yes, I do sometimes wonder what one does with one's age. At my great aunt's 97th birthday dinner party, we began to ask one another questions around the restaurant table: What was your favorite year? What year would you like to forget? Which was the hardest birthday for you? Which birthday was the best?

Everyone had different answers, and it was both fun and insightful to hear their responses ("the last day I was twenty-nine"; "the last year of my marriage"; "the first year with a grandchild"; "the day I started my new job"). Endless responses, none more right than wrong. Yet each of us were watching the days, weeks, months, and years slipping by as we prepared for whatever lies ahead. My favorite answer was from a newly retired sixty-five-year-old who laughingly replied, "My best days are yet to come; I've only just begun and I don't know where life is taking me."

It reminded me of a conversation I once had with my friend Daniel. He had just returned from a vacation in the hills of Georgia. He, like my sister, became lost on some back road. Fortunately, he came upon an elderly woman who was sitting in a rocking chair on the front porch of her house. He stopped and told her where he wanted to go, looking for directions.

"Can you help me out?" he asked.

"Why sure," she replied confidently as she rocked away. "See, here's what you need to do. You just follow this here road a ways, and then when you feels like you're almost there, just stop and you *asks* somebody."

She then nonchalantly leaned over her chair, spit her chewing tobacco out of the side of her mouth with a well-practiced aim into the strategically placed spittoon, and kept on rocking. Daniel and I later laughed over her directions, but then on a more serious note we remarked on the wisdom of this elderly woman. So often in life, that's exactly how we get from Here to There. We just go along until it feels like we're almost There, and then we stop and ask: Are we There yet? How close is Far Away? Have we left Here on our way to over There? Or are we still on the road to There?

And every time, the answer is always the same: "You just goes along until it feels like you're almost there, and then you stop and you *asks* somebody."

By the way, my sister who couldn't find her way lo' so many years ago, went zip-lining the other day to cross one more thing off her bucket list at age 70. ("Just walk to the edge, drop right off, tuck and zip," her instructor told her.) That's one way certainly to get from Here to There!

. . . .

"Would you tell me, please, which way I ought to go from here?"
"That depends a good deal on where you want to get to."
"I don't much care where—"
"Then it doesn't matter which way you go."

—Lewis Carroll

This Is What 60 or 70
or 80 Looks Like

A few years ago, I went to a yoga retreat center to study with my favorite teacher. When the yogi asked me—as he asks all of the attendees at the beginning of each workshop—why I was there, I wondered what I might say that was different or new.

"Next month, I will be sixty years old," I gulped in confession. "I am here to embrace and love myself into sixty."

The yogi nodded his head and gently responded, "Next month you will be sixty."

No, no, no. I was there to embrace *my* being able to say that I would be sixty. I had not come to hear *someone else* say that I would be sixty!

You see, it was the first time that I had ever been sixty. I never envisioned that I would one day be sixty. As one friend told me a few years back when her husband reached this milestone, "I don't mind that he's turning sixty. I just never imagined that I would be married to anyone who was sixty."

Well, today not only am I married to someone seventy-plus, but I am now seventy! When I was fresh out of college and teaching second grade, I naively thought that anyone over the age of thirty was, well . . . old. And sixty or older? Then you were really, really, really old. (And someone please tell me how AARP can begin stalking you at fifty, and then send out a congratulatory note when you turn fifty-five! Is this legal?)

Back then, if you began teaching at age twenty-one and taught for thirty years, you could retire in your early fifties. Not too soon after, you would begin to smell like my late grandmother (who wore Chantilly as her fragrance of choice), jiggle when you walked, and wear false teeth that you took out at night and put in that glass of water by your bed. You had that funny blue rinse in your hair to hide the gray; wore support hose to cover your varicose veins; and you carried a big pocketbook stuffed with cough drops, rubbing liniment, S&H Green Stamps, penny candy, a tube of ruby red lipstick, a compact with mirror, and a monogrammed lace-trimmed handkerchief. Social Security, senior citizen housing, and a tombstone could not be far off.

That's what I thought before I finally could even embrace being sixty. It took me awhile but my understanding and image of what it means to be a senior citizen have changed dramatically: I still am working, have all of my own teeth, go stocking-less, retired to the South where the weather is kinder, and wear my pedometer to get in the required 10,000 steps per day.

Then came the day that I finally began to use my senior discount card for the MTA in New York City. (I did the math: a senior reduced fare was half the base fare and, well, I would be foolish *not* to take the discount.) I've even swallowed my pride and now ask for the senior discount at movie theaters and restaurants. I gladly take the seat on the subway when some young person offers it to me; believe Social Security and Medicare are well-earned benefits; prefer the early-bird specials (smaller portions and less expensive); and enjoy the early boarding offered for seniors on Amtrak. Oh, and those AARP discounts? Let me tell you, they are the bomb!

Someone once said that "I thought 'da' nile' was a river in Africa until I saw the truth." Yes, my friends, I was certainly in denial. Truth be told, I am now a senior citizen, and with that comes privileges and benefits which I gladly accept!

Because I entered kindergarten at age four (they did that back then), most of my friends are older than I am and have been waiting eagerly to welcome me into the world of the seventies. We are one another's role models on how to age with grace and good humor, and we are promised that it will only get better.

To quote one of my "she-roes," Gloria Steinem, in response to a reporter who commented that she did not look her age at forty—and who has gloriously embraced her eighties: "We've been lying for so long, who would know?" (She also replied once when I complimented her on her hair color, "Really? I have so many colors in there; I have no idea *what* color it is.") Only our hairdressers know for sure. Another privilege of growing older!

And, ahem, happy birthday to my two Pisces sisters (March babies), from your middle Scorpio sister.

. . . .

"Fifty was a shock, because it was the end of the center period of life. But once I got over that, sixty was great. Seventy was great. And I loved, I seriously loved aging."

—Gloria Steinem

Trust Me

We had just returned from a visit to the assisted living facility to look at a one-bedroom unit. Ever since my great aunt moved into her two-bedroom, two-bath villa in this senior living community three years ago, we have laughingly referred to the facility as "the big house." An excellent facility and reasonably priced, they offered around-the-clock care, three meals a day, recreational activities, and what seemed like endless outings. Part of the reason we selected this particular housing arrangement was that it would be easier to provide her more care over time.

Unfortunately, on the first night of my visit with her, we ended up in the emergency room until 4:30 a.m., after she fell in the bathroom in the middle of night and thought she had broken her shoulder. Thank goodness, nothing was broken, but it was becoming increasingly apparent that she needed more care and attention. As a concession to me, she had agreed at least to look at the unit. Now back in her villa, I was sitting beside her on the couch, patiently waiting for her evaluation.

"Everyone is so old over there," she said, shaking her head and shuddering.

I quietly reminded her that with her birthday, at the time, coming up in less than a month when we would celebrate her 98th year, she most likely would be the OLDEST person in the facility.

"You know what I mean," she whispered conspiratorially. "They're just so o-l-d."

God love her, my great aunt's vim and vinegar have kept her young at heart, and we should all take notes on how this four-foot, eleven-inch and barely 110-pound woman is living her life so fully and with such determination. Holding tightly to her walker as she scurries around her

7

apartment, Life Alert swinging from a cord around her neck, her age is none of her business . . . nor mine nor anyone else's, apparently (although she has quietly confessed that she no longer buys green bananas).

I remember when I turned thirty and was spending the night with her and my great uncle. She happened by the bathroom as I prepared for bed.

"No night cream on your face?" she asked with eyebrows raised.

"No, why?" I responded.

"Trust me," was all she said as she walked by.

And so, I began my nightly routine of washing my face with Neutrogena and then liberally applying Ponds cold cream (which my grandmother used so that's what I decided to use). Religiously, every night the same routine. When I was approaching forty and had come for a visit, she interrupted my nightly routine with eyebrows raised yet again, asking, "Aren't you applying it to your neck too?"

To my inquiry of why, she once again simply replied, "Trust me."

Over the years, through her gentle prodding, I have added hands and feet to moisturize daily, still using my Ponds. Indeed, I've been known on business trips to hurriedly hop in a cab or order a car service or take a quick walk to the nearest drugstore to purchase a forgotten jar of Ponds. Ponds in the morning, Ponds when I come home from work, and Ponds before I go to bed. Always Ponds, generously applied after washing my face and then brushing and flossing my teeth.

I'm not so sure that she is still moisturizing her face and neck at night, but I do know that she still goes to her weekly manicure and hair appointments, and that her new nightly routine now includes consuming three homemade Butterfinger cookies, accompanied by her scotch on the rocks with a splash of water to wash down the cookies. She keeps a stash of three zipped plastic bags of baked cookies stored in her freezer, making sure that her supply lasts until the next baking venture. And there is always plenty of scotch on hand. (See end of reflection for the cookie recipe. I will leave it up to you on choice of beverage to wash them down.)

Yep, she has emphatically put her petite size-six foot down, and said she's not moving. Not now, not ever. Not in her lifetime if she has anything to say about it. End of discussion.

Because over in "the big house," they are all just so *o-l-d*. And so, here I sit on the couch next to her, waiting for her to cock her head, arch her eyebrows, and say to me yet again, "Trust me."

· · · · · · · · · · · ·

"The idea is to die young as late as possible."

—Ashley Montagu

Betsy's Butterfinger Cookies

Ingredients:

- 1 3/4 cups all-purpose flour
- 3/4 teaspoon baking soda
- 1/4 teaspoon salt
- 3/4 cup granulated sugar
- 1/2 cup salted butter, softened
- 1 large egg, at room temperature
- 8 fun-sized Butterfinger candy bars, chopped

Directions:

1. Preheat oven to 375°F.
2. Combine flour, baking soda, and salt in small bowl and set aside. With an electric mixer, beat sugar and butter until creamy. Beat in egg until just combined.
3. Gradually beat in flour mixture. Stir in Butterfinger pieces by hand. The dough will be very thick. Drop by slightly rounded tablespoons onto ungreased baking sheet.
4. Bake for 10–12 minutes or until lightly browned. Allow to cool on the baking sheets for 5 minutes, then transfer to a wire rack to cool completely.
5. Make-ahead tip: Cookies stay fresh covered at room temperature for up to one week. Baked cookies freeze well—up to three months. Unbaked cookie dough balls freeze well—up to three months. Bake frozen cookie dough balls for an extra minute, no need to thaw.

It's a Little Difficult,
But We Must Learn

I had only been living in New York City for about a year when I was stopped one day on a subway platform by an elderly Eastern European couple. Seeking directions in a language clearly not his own, I surprisingly could help him out (having only ventured on the R for the first four months and then finally learning the Lexington Line before moving to the Seventh Avenue Line, not daring yet to try any of those other "alphabet" lines).

"Just take this subway to 42nd Street, and then follow the signs for the shuttle, which you will take over to the west side to catch the No. 2 or 3 to 72nd Street," I advised him with some confidence.

He nodded in appreciation while his wife clung to his arm with teary eyes. He patted her hand and whispered reassuringly in halted English, "It's a little difficult but we must learn."

His words of encouragement have inspired me for now thirty-plus years: It's a little difficult but we must learn.

I recalled those words last week when my beloved decided that not only must I move from Earthlink and Microsoft Office to Gmail and the Mac, but also to do away with cable TV and use instead Apple TV, Hulu, and Netflix . . . a range of decisions all put into action within seventy-two hours. Yep, I had entered technology purgatory!

Listen, I spent the last thirty years working in a corporation or in a not-for-profit where there was always a knowledgeable IT department. All you had to do was call them up and say "Help" and someone was on the way. I did not need to know *how* things worked. I just needed to know *how to call* someone who knew how things worked.

For problems and mishaps that I did not even know how to describe ("I can't begin to tell you what's wrong, I just know I used to be able to send emails and now I can't"), no sooner than I had hung up the phone, some wonderfully knowledgeable person would magically appear and voilá, my computer was fixed! Alas, retirement does not offer a "technology genie" unless you pay an annual retainer fee like my sister does: this guy drives over to her house and fixes it every time she calls him. Smart woman.

While my beloved was trying to show me how to convert my Earthlink address book to an Excel file to export, and then how to save and retrieve documents on a Mac, and oh yes, how to find the programs I used to enjoy watching on cable now on my Apple TV, and etc., etc., etc., I could actually feel my hair turning gray as I thought to myself that at this rate I was going to need a color touch up weekly rather than my usual every six weeks! (You did hear me when I told you that we did this all within seventy-two hours, right?)

I've heard that you can't teach an old dog new tricks, but I refuse to accept that I am *that* old and I know that I am not a dog. Besides, I have as my inspiration, my Great Aunt Reigh, who lived to the ripe old age of 96, God rest her soul. I remember visiting her one morning out in rural Ohio when she was about 92 years old. I found her not only smoking a cigarette, but also drinking coffee laced with Harvey's Bristol Cream and eating a slice of cherry pie for breakfast.

"Go on, say something," she dared me as she puffed on her cigarette, sitting at the kitchen table in her bathrobe. "Just say something."

"Not me," I said, hands shooting up involuntarily to ward off her unexpected verbal attack. "It all seems to be working for you. Have some more pie."

This same great aunt became so intrigued with fax machines that on one hot summer day in the mid-1990s, she had me drive her down to the local Mom and Pop store (with a two-pump filling station) located on some gravel back road which happened to have a fax machine—all so that she could have someone send her a fax and she could see how it worked. By cracky, if Aunt Reigh could learn how to use a fax machine at ninety-two years of age, smoke cigarettes, drink coffee laced with Harvey's Bristol Cream, *and* eat cherry pie for breakfast, then I know I can figure out how to use a Mac and an Apple TV. Besides, I have a framed needlepoint hanging on my wall—lovingly made and presented to me, from my dear high school friend Marty on the occasion of my receiving my doctorate eons ago—that reads "Learning Never Ends."

As Richelle Goodrich indignantly admonishes us all in *Making Wishes*: "Who told you it was too late? And more importantly, why did you choose to believe them?"

Yes, it may be a little difficult but we must always continue to learn. And, scouts honor, I promise to learn how to use my new Mac and Apple TV . . . sooner rather than later. Meanwhile, I'm inviting all prayers to get me out of this temporary technology purgatory and accepting all contributions for my anticipated monthly hair coloring.

. . . .

"Never stop dreaming,
never stop believing,
never give up,
never stop trying, and
never stop learning."

—Roy T. Bennett, *The Light in the Heart*

The Better to Hear
You, My Dear

Ever since I was about seven years old, I have had to wear glasses, being frightfully nearsighted with astigmatism (you know it's bad when you have to find your glasses on the bed stand before you can read the time on the clock). I was so grateful when they finally made lenses that were thin enough that I didn't have thick eyeglasses *and* I could afford them.

Fifteen years ago, I had Lasik eye surgery and it felt like I was in Steve Martin's movie *Leap of Faith* as he laid hands on me, crying out "Healed, you can see!" Oh, I still needed readers for the fine print, but gosh did I enjoy picking up a variety of inexpensive reading glasses (+2.00) at three for $25. Lately, however, I have begun to notice that I was squinting to read the type on my electronic devices and finally resigned myself to purchasing readers at +2.25.

The better to see you, my dear.

Over the past couple of years, I could also tell that my hearing was not as acute as it had been. What convinced me finally to have my ears checked was the evening I was out to dinner with a mentee of mine. While having dessert and coffee, I thought I heard her say, "I've decided that I would like to have a boat."

I began to wonder how I could help her find a boat—and by the way, when did she become interested in sailing?—and I asked her as much. To which she placed her hand over her heart, gulped, and replied, "I said

---

Portions of this essay first appeared as "Can You Hear Me Now?," in *Meeting God Day By Day* (Cincinnati, OH: Forward Movement, 2014). Used with permission.

that I've decided that I would like to have a beau . . . not a boat. "But," she continued, "I am more distressed that you think it is more likely that I will get a *boat* than a *beau!*"

Well, that urgently took me off to my ear, nose, and throat doctor who in turn referred me to an audiologist, and we learned that I do have a slight hearing loss in BOTH ears. I no longer hear some of the higher ranges, which is where the consonants are (hence hearing boat, not beau). No need for a hearing aid yet, I was reassured; this seems to be one of the natural occurrences of getting older.

I dutifully reported back to my beloved. "It seems that we are both vindicated. You say that I am not listening. I say that I cannot hear you. And guess what? We are both right!!!"

The better to hear you, my dear.

When I still lived in Brooklyn, I would take a long, leisurely walk at least three mornings a week. One Saturday morning, I was walking along Furman Street in a slight summer drizzle when I saw an older gentleman ahead of me. He was facing the Promenade, looking up, with his arms spread wide open. Suddenly, he began to hug himself while doing a little jig, and he seemed to be shouting to himself.

I slowed down, not sure what to do because after all it was New York City, and you can never be too careful, but he seemed to be actually happy. As I came closer, he smiled at me and gleefully shouted, "I just called out 'I don't even know if there is a God' as I raised my fists up to the sky. And just then that beautiful woman up there with an umbrella stopped, looked down, and began to wave at me."

I looked up and there indeed was a pretty young lady with an umbrella who was smiling and waving at both this gentleman and now me. And we waved back.

"Any time a pretty lady waves at an old man like me," he declared with a big smile on his face, "I *know* there is a God."

And so, my dear friends, please be assured that God can hear you— and she is listening.

. . . .

"Grandmother, what big ears you have!"
"All the better to hear with, my child."
—Brothers Grimm, *Little Red Riding Hood*

Calluses and Lip Gloss

Small calluses are forming on the inside of my right index finger and thumb. At first, I wondered what caused this new roughness. Have I forgotten to use hand cream?

And then I remembered . . . it's a callus from writing so much! Constant journaling is creating calluses on my fingers. It has been so long since I had this roughness at the bend of my digits from my graduate school days. With a secretary or administrative assistant for many of my working years—and with personal computers and electronic devices—I had no calluses. Maybe cramps in fingers or threat of carpal tunnel, but no calluses.

No weekly manicures and pedicures either; now treating myself only every two or three weeks. I knew that my feet were not as soft and tender as they have been in the past, but now I wonder about my hands. No more maintenance and running in and out within an hour at the nail salon. It's at least two and perhaps three hours for an appointment. I give an extra generous tip to the manicurist for her hard work each time I see her.

I recall studying one of my friend's husband's snarled fingers that are covered with calluses. An esteemed scholar and prolific writer, his right hand represented his years of sitting at a desk—writing, thinking, gnawing on his knuckles. Will mine become as noticeable over time?

I am thinking of a classmate in a wheelchair whom I came to know while at Harvard on a fellowship I enjoyed the year after I retired. I never saw her wearing shoes. She only wore socks. I admired how she would hold a pen between her big toe and her second toe on a foot covered with

Portions of this essay first appeared as "Callused Prayers," in *Seeking God Day By Day* (Cincinnati, OH: Forward Movement, 2013). Used with permission.

a sock, writing—quickly and clearly—in the notebook propped on a chair angled to the right of her. I wondered how she kept her feet warm and dry in the winter months. Now I begin to wonder if the young lady in my class had calluses on the toes of her right foot.

The last time I visited New York City, there was a street fair in my old neighborhood. A new health-conscious pharmacy was giving out samples of vitamins and herbs. The young lady looked at me carefully and then handed me a vitamin packet for "50 plus." Do I look 50 plus? What does 50 plus look like any ol' way? And by the way, what does 60 plus look like? How about 70 plus?

I made a small purchase at this same pharmacy, and their makeup artist offered to give me a free makeover. Do I look like I need a makeover as well? No, thank you. I wore make up for thirty years. Lip gloss and a little mascara is all that I need today, especially now that I am retired.

. . . .

"I like the woman you became better than the girl you were. I like the story you've written on your face."

—Joanna Bourne

Where's Joseph?

This past week, I spent most of my time decorating our home, bringing down boxes marked "Christmas," unpacking the tissue paper while oo-ing and ah-ing over forgotten treasures, and playing my favorite holiday music (Johnny Mathis, Nat King Cole, BeBe and CeCe Winans) to fill the rooms with the excitement of Christmas. It is the sure sign that Christmas is coming when I bring out the nativity scene.

About fifteen years ago, as a gift to myself, I ordered a very special hand-crafted nativity set. When it arrived, I eagerly unpacked the pieces and assembled them for display. Much to my surprise, I had Mary, Joseph, an angel, and two sheep, but no wise men! When I went on the website, I realized that I needed to order each of the three wise men separately.

I shared my dilemma with a colleague at work, who only remarked somewhat indignantly, "Have you noticed the nativity scene down in our lobby? There's no Baby Jesus?!"

I explained to him that in some traditions, the Baby Jesus does not appear until Christmas Eve.

"I don't care what you say," he replied. "I'm from the South; and in the South, we have a Baby Jesus!"

Which got me to thinking: did I have a baby Jesus? I rushed home to carefully examine my newly acquired nativity scene. Sure enough, there was baby Jesus in the arms of Mary. But I had no cradle. I was reluctant to go back on the website to see if I had to order the cradle separately. Hey, I've now got three wise men, Mary, Joseph and baby Jesus, what

Portions of this essay first appeared as "Jesus Is the Reason," in *Seeking God Day By Day* (Cincinnati, OH: Forward Movement, 2013). Used with permission.

more did I need? And to this day, I have no cradle for Baby Jesus. I've added a shepherd, several more sheep, a camel, and the creche . . . but no cradle.

So, this year, as I carefully unwrapped the figurines, I realized I didn't have Joseph. I had his staff (which has kept falling from his left hand since the initial purchase) but no Joseph. Somewhere, I have this distant memory of finding Joseph after everything was stored away last year and putting it a very safe place for the next year. For the life of me, I can't remember where that safe place is!

This comes with getting older. We put something down or away, and then can't remember where. My friend Diane reassured me, "Oh, honey, it happens to all of us. If it cost under $20, just buy another one and quit fretting."

Unfortunately, one can't purchase Joseph solo; he comes with Mary, baby Jesus, an angel, and two sheep—all for much more than $20. Besides, then Joseph would be a bigamist! Poor Mary, already the immaculate conception and now about to become a single parent. In this age of #MeToo, with more and more men disappearing as women step up to the forefront, well maybe this is the #MeToo moment for Mary.

But I'm not giving up. Somewhere there is a Joseph waiting to be found and set in his rightful place.

. . . .

"If you wish to forget anything on the spot, make a note that this thing is to be remembered."

—Edgar Allan Poe

One Leg at a Time

M y great aunt fell again. She fell a month ago in her apartment with someone not even a foot away. That time, there was a deep gash on her forehead with lots of blood. This time, they suspect she broke her thumb, but at her age, they recommended that we do nothing for fear a resetting of the bone might prove to be fatal. She has her walker (which we've nicknamed her "truck"), but all too often she tries to get around without it.

Her frequency of falling and the breaking of bones (hip, collar bone, ribs) is what prompted the family to insist that she move out of her house into independent living three years ago. Once in the apartment and after falling in the tub several times, and another time in the kitchen when the glass carafe shredded around her, I finally convinced her to actually *wear* the Life Alert around her neck and not use it as a toy for her cats. Well, that and my demanding that she sign a statement that she refused to wear her Life Alert and therefore if she were found dead on the floor—having bled to death and her hungry cats beginning to eat her—it was of her own choice! A little cold, I know, but it worked.

Having good balance is key to preventing potentially disabling falls; and it is a medical fact that our gait changes with aging. The goal is to keep walking as long as possible, and weight-bearing exercises are encouraged. Personally, I ride my bike, take water aerobics classes, practice yoga, and enjoy long walks . . . but even with all of this, I still find myself, at times, unsteady on my feet.

My friend Lucia, who is an amazing personal trainer, always asks her baby boomer clients—as part of the initial assessment—what they want to be able to continue to do. One said to raise her arms above her head to be able to put her carry-on luggage in the overhead on the plane; another said to be able to lift and carry her toddler grandchild. When I thought about it, I realized that I wanted to be able to swing my right leg over the two-foot-high jacuzzi tub. (I'm okay with the left leg, but my tight ab abductor on the right sometimes proves to be a challenge. Ouch!) Not that I use that tub much anymore, indeed I would need to pole vault into that tub! But it does need to be cleaned now and then. And I use my right leg to get on and off my bike, not as high a swing but still a lift.

I must confess that when my daughter or my younger friends want to "help" me out of the car or up from kneeling at the pew in church, I politely—and sometimes not so politely—brush aside the offered hand. Appreciate the consideration, but I got this. Honest. At least for today. I need to be able to get up and down on my own as long as possible.

I heard once that if you can put one pant leg on while still freestanding on the other leg, you are doing pretty good. I always find myself chuckling when on some days I find it to be easy peasy, while on other days I need to hold onto a door knob or just sit down to pull those pant legs up.

Meanwhile, I will stay faithful to my own exercise routine, always praying to be upright, steady, and mobile as long as possible . . . before I too am considered a fall risk.

. . . .

"I love living. I love that I'm alive to love my age. There are many people who went to bed just as I did yesterday evening and didn't wake this morning. I love and feel very blessed that I did."
—Maya Angelou

2

The Storms of Life

Let It Be Kind to You

Whatever bad things have happened to you in your life, whatever hard things you've been through, you have to do three things. You have to accept it. You have to be kind to it . . . And . . . you have to let it be kind to you," wrote Kerry Egan, a hospital chaplain, in a collection of stories about some of her patients.* I have been mulling over Egan's words.

It's been an interesting past seven months, witnessing my own transition from living and working in New York City for thirty-one years to retiring and joining my beloved in our home down south. Alongside that happy fact, I contracted shingles around my eye and then in my eye in May; Hurricane Matthew destroyed our master suite in early October, sending us to a series of hotel rooms before we found a temporary rental apartment; and we were the victim of a hit-and-run accident that totaled our car in early November.

My sister teasingly told me that I was a lot like a young Harry Potter who, as a new wizard with his wand, did not quite know how to use his power yet. I wanted to do some renovations to the house, so five huge oak trees fell on the house. I wanted a new car, so ours was totaled. "Don't you pray anymore, let me pray for you until you can get a better handle on how to pray," she chided me. "We know your prayers will be answered, but it would seem that you still need to work on your technique."

Throughout it all, I have been able to accept most of the "bad things" with deep gratitude and by counting my blessings: I have terrific doctors and no permanent damage to my vision; we have excellent insurance

---

*Kerry Egan, *On Living* (New York: Riverhead Books, 2016), 8.

and will have a practically brand-new house inside and out; no one was injured in either the hurricane or the car collision; and we now have a brand-new SUV.

But how to let all of the bad stuff be *kind* to me?! Hmmm.

I shared my dilemma recently with my physician during an annual checkup, and he wisely observed, "I guess it's easier to accept bad things when you know the outcome will be good. For example, you knew you were going to get better and your shingles would go away; you knew you would eventually have a beautifully renovated house; and you needed a new car anyway and could afford to buy one. Therefore, no matter how inconvenienced you were or are, you remained optimistic."

So now I wonder, maybe we're talking about hope here: a hope and a belief that, as the old folks used to say, "it will all work itself out." I do not wish to imply that hope is to be correlated with financial currency, but rather this is a hope of faith currency, believing that all things work together for the good to them that love God, to them who are called according to his purpose (Romans 8:28 [KJV]). And for many of us, sadly we tend to leave out the *called according to his purpose*, which for me is the most important part of that verse.

Still, I think I am much better able to let situations and things be kind to me than I am able to let the actions of other people be kind to me. Quite honestly, it's people that I have the most trouble with—like former colleagues, so-called friends, news commentators, and yes, even some newly elected or appointed officials. How do I let all that bad stuff inflicted upon me by other people . . . however can I let *that* kind of stuff . . . be kind to me?

Don't know. Not sure. But it most likely has something to do with love. Ugh. Oh, that *love* thing again, including loving those enemies who have despitefully used and misused me.

Well, I have never suggested that I was following in the footsteps of Bishop Tutu or the Dalai Lama. So please be patient with me; God is not through with me yet!

· · · · · · · · · · · ·

"Charity . . . appears as a huge demand on the will to continue to think positively of, and act generously towards, others; and especially the [expletive], whoever they may be."
—James Alison

Spanx or Squirrels?

I received an urgent voicemail from a dear friend, "You have to call me when you get a moment. I have something to tell you that I can only share with you."

Returning the call immediately, she began to tell me what I am sure was a hilarious story about trying to climb into her Spanx so that she could put on a particular dress to go out to dinner that night. I don't own any Spanx, that wonderful slimming intimate that holds everything in and prevents anything from jiggling. Cottage cheese thighs disappear; muffin waists are sucked in; and derrières get lifted. I probably should get some Spanx.

As I listened to her struggles of pulling and tugging, all I could think about were the squirrels that had begun to make their home in our attic. With only tenuous structure remaining on which the contractors could secure the very large tarps thrown over our roof while we await renovations from October's hurricane, the squirrels had found a nice place to make their home. I'm sure there is a Walt Disney movie in the making up there; they seem to be rehearsing their song and dance routines day and night.

Friends have recommended glue traps, fresh blood, and something called "Critter Ridder." Seeking a more humane solution, my beloved already has caught five squirrels in some sort of trap using peanut butter on a cracker as bait, and then driven the rascals over the bridge into new territory. (He swears that squirrels can't swim across the Intracoastal Waterway.) I'm just hoping that by the time the reconstruction has been completed, the squirrels will have figured out that this is not their new, permanent abode.

So, I guess I was feeling neither very magnanimous nor compassionate about my friend's Spanx dilemma while contending with the squirrels in our attic. Research suggests that with frequent and intimate exposure to tragedy, one can experience something called "compassion fatigue." Hmmm, let's see: shingles, hurricane, car totaled, and squirrels in attic. Oh, yes, and in our temporary apartment there have been three (count them three) major leaks within four days in the bathroom and kitchen ceilings that have awakened us in the middle of the night—leaks from two different apartments above us, no less. Certainly, none of this was tragic but it sure feels frequent and intimate.

Maybe I will buy myself some Spanx after all. It might help me become more compassionate about the ordinary, everyday occurrences in life and restore some semblance of a sense of humor. And maybe, just maybe, my beloved will take me out to dinner tonight for Valentine's Day, if I can squeeze back into that little black knit dress that has been hanging in my closet for far too long.

· · · · · · · · · · · ·

"My mission in life is not merely to survive, but to thrive; and to do so with some passion, some compassion, some humor, and some style."

—Maya Angelou

Fences, Borders, and Walls

I remember when I first moved to the Bay Area in the late 1970s, people would ask me where I was from. When I told them that I hailed from Ohio, they would respond, "Oh, that's where you all don't have fences, the yards just go from one to another." Until then, I had not ever really thought about fences between yards. Yes, we had hedges and trees to create natural borders (always with a pathway somewhere to allow you to slip through easily to your neighbor), but rarely did one see a fence. Having lived in apartment buildings in major cities for the past forty years, fences were not required: there were bricks, cement, and mortar to keep us apart.

I didn't think much more about fences again until after Hurricane Matthew, when ten tall oak and pine trees fell on our property, including three that fell on our roof, right on top of each other! (The structural engineer asked our contractor if the three trees fell all at the same time or at different times, to which our contractor replied dryly, "We don't know, we weren't here.") I had prayed that none of the trees on *our* property would fall on our house. None did. They were our neighbors' trees. The lesson here: Pray BIG and WIDE.

In an effort to assist residents with the timely removal of damaged trees, our community association temporarily relaxed the requirement for tree removal, and permits were not required for thirty days. My beloved quickly had twenty trees removed from our property. All trees that looked like they could fall and do any kind of damage . . . ever in our lifetime . . . were cut down and taken away expeditiously. Days of stump removal and the sounds of stump grinding permeated our property, while I gritted my teeth and stuffed my ears with cotton.

And so now our landscape has changed dramatically. There is no privacy from our neighbors' homes. I can look into their kitchen windows and they can look into ours. Gone are the beautiful moss-covered trees with palmettos tucked between to create natural and graceful privacy. We need borders.

Yikes! Did I just write that? We need borders!!!??? Yes, we need something that would make us feel a little less exposed and provide a little more privacy. We need something that would bring back the natural beauty of our home and neighborhood. No longer is there any kind of blending on our stretch of the neighborhood. Homes around us stand in stark relief, largely unadorned by nature.

In Charles Maier's book, *Once Within Borders: Territories of Power, Wealth, and Belonging Since 1500*, he asks readers to consider the many ways in which human societies have claimed borders and territories to consolidate power, wealth, and group affiliation—and how those borders have shaped people's consciousness through time. Further, the lack of borders in cyberspace has changed the dynamic completely, and Maier wonders to what degree our societies have moved toward a post-territorial world. Well, I can tell you that, in our household and our neighbors' households, we are *not* post-territorial. We still need and want borders!

"Good fences make good neighbors," Robert Frost suggested in his poem "Mending Wall." I'm not so sure about fences, or walls, or even territories in the world today, but I do know that we will be planting Podocarpus, Tuscan Blue Rosemary, and Ligustrum shrubs to create natural privacy borders around our home. It won't be a wall, cost billions of dollars, and unlike the Great Wall of China will not take 2,000 years to build, nor will it be impassable, but it certainly will be beautiful!

· · · · · · · · · · · ·

"Love thy neighbor: yet don't pull down your hedge."

—Benjamin Franklin

No More Bad News

I don't know about you, but I am exhausted by the constant barrage of bad news: natural disasters; tragedies; a shooting rampage; massive security breaches; and tweets, counter-tweets, and more tweets. I am almost afraid to wake up in the morning to turn on the television or check digital news feeds or read the most recent tweets. It all seems like just too much right now and I am beginning to feel at a loss as to how or if I can make a difference.

And then I remembered a past trip to Panama on a mission trip with Trinity Wall Street of New York City. Fifteen volunteers began in Panama City but then took a small plane over to Changuinola, a city in the Bocas del Toro Province of Panama. An island only about thirty-seven square miles with a population of about 31,000, Changuinola is a tropical city surrounded by banana plantations. This region in the Anglican Province of Panama has only one deacon who serves four congregations and a presbyter who visits once a month.

We spent the first day at San Miguel Arcangel Episcopal Church located near the border of Guabito where we helped paint the exterior and install the ceiling of the interior temple, providing much-needed insulation. On the second day, we went to the Transfiguration Church in Changuinola to work on the Parish Hall, a space used for Sunday school and church meetings. A deteriorated screen and iron bars on the windows had been replaced with sturdier materials but now needed to be painted.

The rusted screening had been cut away, that is all but about a one-inch border around each of the windows. Behind the old screening and covering the windows was the new metal screening, framed by wood—all of which needed to be painted black. There was to be no scraping,

priming, or sanding—just painting over the rust, over the rough surfaces, and onto the new metal mesh screening, inside and out. Black.

My beloved and two other women besides myself made up this team
(the others staying behind to complete the work at San Miguel), and we
were joined by one parishioner. Our supplies were four paint brushes,
one roller, two paint pans, and one ladder. The brush that I was given
was a two-inch trim brush; the other three brushes were four inches.
The brushes were new—like the metal screening—and we were there to
serve, not to complain, so I started painting.

My work was slow and tedious. In order for the paint to adhere,
it needed to be applied thickly on the rusted screen border, and with a
two-inch trim brush, my strokes did not cover much. My beloved used
the ladder to reach the upper windows, and the rest of us worked below.
Standing in the heat of the sun of this tropical rainforest—even with
a hat, a long-sleeve blouse, gloves, and sunglasses—I quickly became
drenched in my own perspiration, taking short breaks to drink bottled
water and to cool off before the lone fan.

Slap, slap, slap, dip for paint, more slap, slap, slap. Out of the corner
of my eye, I could see that the other volunteers were able to cover the
screening much more quickly with their larger brushes and the single
roller. I steadfastly stayed focused on the task, choosing to make this
my "Brother Lawrence moment," the Carmelite monk (1614–1691) who
taught us in *Practicing the Presence of God* how to find the divine in the
simplest of acts. Brother Lawrence wrote: "We ought not to be weary of
doing little things for the love of God, who regards not the greatness of
the work, but the love with which it is performed."*

At noon, we ran out of paint, and we welcomed the break until we
realized—after eating our lunch prepared for us and another hour had
passed—that the parish had no money to buy more paint. We three
women volunteers piled into a car driven by a congregant to go into town
to buy more black paint. By the end of the day, the screening had been
painted inside and out, the local parishioners were pleased, and we were
happy but exhausted.

---

*Brother Lawrence, *The Practice of the Presence of God* (Cincinnati, OH:
Forward Movement Publications, 2002), 22

So maybe it wasn't the right kind of paint, and we didn't prepare the surfaces, and we aren't even sure how long these new paint jobs will last. We tried to do something to make a difference, however, and it was something that they wanted and needed—not necessarily how we might have wanted to give. Most importantly, it was all done in love.

You don't have to go to Panama, or Puerto Rico, or Mexico City, or Paradise, California, or . . . (you fill in the blank). You can just look around where you are and see if there is some small act of kindness that you could offer that would make a difference in someone else's life today. Maybe it's as simple as opening a door for another, or saying hello to a stranger, or carrying a package for another, or making that telephone call to an elderly neighbor, or sending a card to a friend. Maybe it is as simple as offering a small act of kindness in love.

Plato is attributed with encouraging us to "be kind; everyone you meet is fighting a hard battle." It certainly seems as though everywhere we look, we are in battle today, and the fighting is *getting* even harder. So, let's just try being kind to one another . . . and stop sharing so much bad news. It's a start.

. . . .

"The bad news is that nothing lasts forever.
The good news is that nothing lasts forever."

—J. Cole

Transitions Yet to Come

It was the last day at my job in Chicago, and I was doing the last-minute things that always make you crazy: answering correspondence; making sure the files were in order; packing up my personal effects. The movers were due at my apartment the following week, and the same hectic routine would have to be repeated there.

Brenda peeked into my office to offer consolation.

"How ya' doin'?" she asked.

Looking up from my many piles and boxes, I grimaced. "Overwhelmed."

"Is it the leaving or the going?" Brenda asked.

I hesitated. Leaving or going? But of course. There is a difference, isn't there? In any transition, there are stages—leaving, going, arriving, and being.

"The leaving," I replied. "Definitely the leaving. I'll work on the going once the movers have come."

Somehow, understanding where I was in the process provided some comfort for me. I'm leaving. Soon, I'll be going. Then I'll be arriving. And finally, finally, I simply will be being.

On the morning of my departure, my great aunt handed me a farewell gift. "Open it now," she said, eyes twinkling, filled with love.

It was a small framed poster on which was written nine simple words: "Lord guide me through the transitions yet to come."

I carefully placed the gift in my carry-on bag. It would be the first thing I unpacked upon my arriving. Today, more than thirty years later,

Portions of this essay first appeared as "In the Meantime," in *Finding God Day By Day* (Cincinnati, OH: Forward Movement, 2010). Used with permission.

the frame is placed prominently in my house: one of the first and last things that I see as I begin and end my day.

This gift prompts me to ask: aren't we all at some time in our lives in transition? We all find ourselves standing in that moment called "in the meantime." It's that "in between" time. While we aren't where we were, we sure aren't where we want to be. We are in transition.

I do not know what your personal circumstances are. I do not know whether you are leaving, or if you are going, or if you are arriving, or if you are just simply . . . being. Nor do I know what you will find waiting for you this week, or next month, or within the next year. Will you stay at your job or will this be the year that you retire? Will you remain in your home or in your town? Will you recover from your health challenge? Nor do I know which stage of the transition you are in on your own life's journey. I do not pretend to know what the answer is for you. I do not *need* to know; while I may not know *what* the answer is, I do know Who holds the answer.

My great aunt is in transition. Sometimes, I wonder if she thinks of this time as leaving or if she thinks of it as going. Does she believe that one day, she will just be being? I don't know. Looking at the gift that she gave me so many years ago, I find reassurance and comfort that everything will be all right someday. Lord, guide me through the transitions yet to come.

. . . .

"Rest in the Lord and wait patiently for Him."

—Psalm 37:7 (KJV)

Stay Safe

S tay safe. That's all I heard or read on the news, in emails, in texts, or on telephone calls last week. Stay safe.

Back when I lived in New York City, we used to say "safe home," wishing the person an uneventful commute home—which indeed could sometimes turn out to be a perilous journey. That was before earthquakes, fires, hurricanes, tropical storms, tornadoes, forced curfews, and mandatory evacuations. Now we say to others "stay safe." Stay safe.

I remember standing in the line at the neighborhood drugstore the day before Hurricane Sandy, a category 2 storm that was hurling its way toward the coast of the northeast. The woman ahead of me was purchasing two six packs of beer. She, laughing, told anyone within ear shot, "I'm from Louisiana; we know how to get through hurricanes and storms!" The young couple behind me had a case of soft drinks in their hands with enough junk food to feed an army.

Comfort. That's what we were all looking for as we awaited the storm that promised to be a doozy. I had been so busy checking off my list of "to do's" to get ready for the hurricane that I had nothing in the apartment that would comfort me. I quickly dropped out of line and grabbed three candy bars, a package of donuts, and a big bag of potato chips, and decided that I would make one last stop on my way home at the corner deli to pick up a bouquet of flowers.

Walking the streets in my Brooklyn neighborhood on October 28, 2012, I saw others in various stages of preparation for the hurricane/

Portions of this essay first appeared as "Sustain and Comfort Us," in *Seeking God Day By Day* (Cincinnati, OH: Forward Movement, 2013). Used with permission.

tropical storm. Young mothers with their toddlers, hoping to get them exhausted by playing outside before they would be cooped up inside for who knows how long; expectant mothers with swollen bellies sitting on stoops with water jugs and overnight bags, waiting for their rides to get them to safer territory; joggers getting in their last-minute runs; animal lovers walking their dogs; and last-minute grocery shoppers loaded down with jugs of water and rolls of paper towels.

But that was before Hurricane Matthew in 2016, when five trees fell on our house in Savannah and we were displaced for seven months while renovations were being completed. Similar to Sandy, I purchased and ate a lot of comfort food during Matthew. This time, as I packed and prepared for Hurricane Irma, I found myself with a sheer loss of appetite. Just the thought of food made me nauseous. So instead, I packed apples, crackers, cheese, protein bars, nuts, and water, plenty of water; there could never be too much water. I was much more focused on gathering insurance policies, social security cards, immunization records, bank account numbers, credit account numbers, and family records. iPads, iPods, chargers, and my password book went into a pouch. I carefully videotaped all rooms, walls, floors, and closets for an inventory, and I moved items off the floor to protect them from possible flooding. I packed clothes and sundries for seven days—not just three days—away.

Then there were the irreplaceable items. The mustard seed necklace that my mother gave me years ago; my father's Bible; the Bible my grandmother gave me when I received my doctorate; three folders marked "special photos"; a piece of my late grandfather Gubby's shirt; my favorite wedding picture still in its frame; and the first pair of earrings my beloved ever bought for me. Finally, I went outside and cut a bloom from the gardenia plant—a plant my beloved had so tenderly nursed back to life after the last hurricane—and pressed it between the pages of my father's Bible.

As we finally got into the car and slowly drove out our driveway, I turned back and whispered to our house, "Stay safe."

. . . .

"The ache for home lives in all of us. The safe place where we can go as we are and not be questioned."

—Maya Angelou

The News May Not Be
Full of Joyful Tidings, But
Merry Christmas Anyway

"The news may not be full of joyful tidings, but the season is still a time to wish you loving greetings for the New Year" was handwritten inside the Christmas card.

My sentiments exactly. What happened to the Good News that we are supposed to be shouting from the mountaintops?

Sometimes, I turn on the television in the morning and feel like Dorothy Parker who supposedly answered the doorbell saying: "What fresh hell is this?" The news, indeed, is not full of joyful tidings, and I turn the television off. During Advent, I have decided to fast from all news and social media; it is too much for my soul to bear. No Sunday *New York Times*, CNN, MSNBC (sorry Rachel Maddow), NPR, *Time* magazine, *Newsweek*, iNews on iPhone or iPad, Facebook, even *People* magazine. None, nada, zip.

I don't really need it. Headlines come my way in extraneous conversations, grocery store lines, coffee hours after church, airport corridors, and especially from my Gen X niece who texts me often from a major southern Ohio grocery store chain that she manages. Thanks to her, I have seen photos of t-shirts, jackets, and signs that proudly and boldly display troubling and sometimes frightening points of view.

Yesterday, my niece sent me her latest text accompanied with photos, lamenting that all the toy dolls of color were still on the shelves, untouched. Barbie dolls, baby dolls, princess dolls . . . all of these beautiful, sweet dolls of color were still in the store. Amber, beige, chocolate, caramel, chestnut, cocoa, coffee, tan, mahogany, black. No one had bought them. One customer even had the audacity to return her previous purchase of three little dolls in a plastic sleeve because one of the dolls was black. "Don't they have any that are all white?" she asked, and requested a refund or store credit.

I sent a text back: "I'll buy ten dolls; please donate them to a homeless shelter where little girls would love to receive a doll like one of these for Christmas." My sister and two friends matched my offer; so now forty dolls of color will come off the shelves and find their way under Christmas trees, no longer dismissed nor unwanted.

Amid less than joyful tidings, I'm not sure what else to do but continue to fast, pray, and wait. And then pray some more. And help to make sure that little girls who look like me have dolls that look like them for Christmas. It hardly seems enough.

. . . .

"The only Good News of glad tidings is the Gospel of Salvation."
                                                              —Lailah Gifty Akita

3
Fighting a Hard Battle

The Gift That Cannot
Be Regifted

Traditionally, people did not take down Christmas trees and other decorations until after Epiphany (January 6), but nowadays we begin to see Christmas trees out on the curb on December 26. Christmas is over; it is time to put the gifts away or return them or exchange them. And then comes the regifting. I don't know about you, but I confess that I usually make three piles of my Christmas gifts: keep, return, regift. (Did you know that there is even a National Regifting Day—an annual observance held each year on the Thursday before Christmas? Amazing.)

I recently went to the Emily Post Institute website to find the protocols for receiving gifts. Rule number one on Ms. Post's list is, when opening a gift in the presence of the giver, to thank the person enthusiastically. Even if the present is the last thing you wanted, thank the giver for his or her thoughtfulness, drawing on the actor in you to mask any disappointment. Be pleasant but non-committal, saying something like: "It's so nice of you to think of me!" or "What a creative choice!" Or my personal favorite: "Oh my, you shouldn't have; no, *really*, you shouldn't have."

Last year, as I sorted my gifts into the requisite three piles, much to my surprise I only had one gift in the regift pile: a very, very expensive gift from someone who has been the bane of my existence. I was holding in my hands this very beautiful gift that had never been used. (I know this because the return receipt was tucked inside with the PRICE of the gift clearly listed.) Trust me; I did not want this gift from that person.

This essay first appeared as "The Gift That Cannot Be Regifted," in Erma Bombeck Writers' Workshop (January 2017). Used with permission.

At Christmas dinner, I had a chance to chat with one of my family "aunties." I told my auntie about the gift and about the giver and how I planned to donate it to the Salvation Army or to Goodwill or perhaps to regift it.

Auntie leaned over and looking me dead in the eye, and said, "You can't give away that gift. That was a gift asking for forgiveness; it was a gift of atonement. You have to keep that gift."

Keep the gift?! Why, I don't think I even want that gift in my house!!! And I told my auntie as much, to which she replied with a knowing smile, "Well, it's a good thing you aren't God then, isn't it?"

Wow! God? The God who forgives me every day—often times more than once a day—who never turns me away? *That* God? Yet there I was, ready to regift something that can be neither returned nor regifted: the gift of love, of mercy, of grace, and of forgiveness.

Let me confess right here that I did *not* keep the very expensive and unexpected gift I received from my nemesis. But just so you know, per Emily Post, I did send the giver a very profuse and genuine handwritten note of thanks. And because I already had this same gift item and did not need it, again according to Emily Post, I could give it to someone else if: 1) I told them that I already have one; and very importantly, 2) it was not gift wrapped.

Yes, that unwanted, extravagant gift I received last Christmas turned out to be one of the best gifts I have ever received because it gave me an opportunity to remember that there is one gift that can never be regifted.

. . . .

"It's one of the greatest gifts you can give yourself, to forgive. Forgive everybody. I mean, we ask the Creator to forgive our stupidest actions. The cruelest mean-hearted things."
—Maya Angelou

Groundhog Day

Every year, we await groundhog handler Ben Hughes and Punxsutawney Phil to determine if we will have an early spring during the annual festivities on February 2 in Punxsutawney, Pennsylvania . . . and every year it seems that winters get colder down south and even colder up north.

"To everything there is a season, a time for every purpose under the heaven" (Ecclesiastes 3:1 [KJV]). This is the season of winter, with brutal commutes and dropping temperatures; for groundhogs ending hibernation and slowly lengthening days; for tissues with aloe and Vicks on the chest; and for melting ice and thawing hearts. Spring promises not to be far away, at least according to my new favorite weather predictor Punxsutawney Phil.

During the year-long fellowship at Harvard I enjoyed after retiring in 2009, I remember looking outside the door of my studio one chilly February morning and seeing piles of dirty snow. I had been trying to figure out why the snow piles never seemed to get smaller. And then that day, I saw my landlord with a wheelbarrow, summarily dumping the snow shoveled from the sidewalks in front of the complex by my entryway. When I inquired, she said it was the only place to put it; and they have been doing it this way for fifteen years. I was reassured that when it melts, it would all go down into the ground. Further, I was not to worry because it wouldn't flood into my apartment. Boston had a recorded 70.7 inches of snow as of early February that year, and I was certain that at least 70 inches had been parked in front of my door!

When I returned to the studio after a week away, I was greeted by a very narrow, icy pathway to my apartment. Two boards had been placed over the ice as a way to get to my steps. The dirty snow pile seemed even higher this time, and it was very difficult to get my suitcase down the steps and into the apartment. It was the first time I had been near tears since arriving in Cambridge. Too upset to have a civil conversation, I waited a day before I mentioned the problem to the landlord, and she promised to clear the entrance way as soon as the ice began to melt.

Friday, February 11 is the anniversary of Nelson Mandela being released from the Victor Verster Prison in Paarl. I remember that I was on holiday with my friend Janet in Saint Martin on that historic day. We sat on the floor in our hotel room, with our door open so that the housekeepers—leaning on mops and brooms—could watch the television from the doorway. Tears flowing down our cheeks, holding hands tightly, Janet and I watched Mandela's first steps to freedom.

When I finally was able to visit South Africa, I had an opportunity to visit Robben Island (where Mandela spent eighteen of his twenty-seven years in prison) and see the conditions under which he had to live. Confined to a small cell, the floor for his bed, a bucket for his toilet, he worked in the quarry which nearly blinded him. I wondered then . . . and still wonder . . . how President Mandela and Bishop Tutu were able to embrace this concept of peace and reconciliation, especially given the horrendous conditions of apartheid; and I am ashamed by my own temptations to harden my heart toward some injustice, big or small.

And so, I did not yell and scream at my landlord for not having a clear pathway that day. Instead, I waited a day before I approached her in a chance meeting outside. Later, I could hear the clanging of the shovel, as she chipped away at the ice and snow to clear a better pathway for me. Even to this day, I wonder: was it the same kind of clanging as might have been heard when Mandela was shoveling a roadway on Robben Island?

• • • • • • • • • • • •

"Resentment and anger are bad for your blood pressure and your digestion."

—Bishop Desmond Tutu

Remember to Love

How quickly the Christmas decorations came down in the stores only to be replaced with the red hearts and cupids for Valentine's Day. Cards are temptingly displayed for all kinds of relationships—family, friends, co-workers, secret admirers, loved ones.

When I was a classroom teacher many years ago, Valentine's Day was my favorite holiday because it required little preparation. All I had to do was set aside an hour for the children to decorate their brown paper bags; tack them up on the bulletin board; instruct the children that every child got a valentine; and buy red Hawaiian punch and make cupcakes with red icing. For the last hour of the classroom day, I'd pass out the bags and goodies . . . and watch.

It would be so quiet that you could hear a pin drop as the children licked the icing off their cupcakes and opened each valentine carefully. An occasional "thank you" was called out for a special valentine.

One Valentine's Day, I went into a card shop and spent forty-five minutes picking out my valentines. Most were easy, until I came to one. It was for a family member, and while I know that blood is thicker than water, it felt pretty thin right then.

And then I remembered the scripture: "And now abideth faith, hope, love, these three; the greatest of these is love" (1 Corinthians 13:13 [KJV]).

Portions of this essay first appeared as "The Greatest of These Is Love," in *Finding God Day By Day* (Cincinnati, OH: Forward Movement, 2010). Used with permission.

I needed to remember to love. I found the perfect Valentine's card for my family member, and thanked God silently for his grace and mercy in my unloving moment.

· · · · · · · · · · · ·

"All you need is love. But a little chocolate now and then doesn't hurt."

—Charles M. Schulz

An Act of Kindness

Watching the weather station, happily ensconced in my home, I still shudder as I watch trucks and cars stalled by winter blasts, and predicted low temperatures forecasted—turning up the heat slightly and buttoning my sweater while indoors. When I lived up North, I used to watch college students dressed skimpily in frigid weather. Was I ever like that? I think so, as I recall my own mother often chiding me to put on my hat and gloves "before I caught my death of cold!"

Pathways on sidewalks were often narrow, with only room enough for one foot step at a time. I envied the much more nimble students who quickly—and laughingly—put one foot in front of the other, balancing easily as if trapeze walking. I even would see them jogging or riding their bikes on those snowy, icy sidewalks and streets. I, on the other hand, would walk more slowly, trying to keep my balance between snow piles of three feet or more.

One week, I found myself pulling and pushing my grocery/laundry cart (which is almost three feet wide), loaded to the top with packages to trek over the narrow, icy path; and it was particularly hazardous. If lucky, there were sections where the sidewalk had been cleared snow-shovel wide—about ten inches—and I was huffing and puffing, tilting the cart on two side wheels, praying the packages would not topple out.

Just then an angel appeared: a young mother (with her son in tow) who offered to help me. She went to the front of the cart and I stayed in the back. Together we were able to lift the cart high above the snow piles and down over the icy, snowy slope to the street. I am sure her previous

Portions of this essay first appeared as "Acts of Kindness," in *Seeking God Day By Day* (Cincinnati, OH: Forward Movement, 2013). Used with permission.

years of navigating a carriage or stroller alone helped her to feel compassion for an older woman with a laundry cart. To my pleasant surprise, she continued to walk with me the final half block, and helped me lift the cart up the steps to the UPS Store. Her son—no more than five years old—patiently followed behind us. I thanked her profusely.

"I try to do at least one nice thing a day," she responded cheerfully. "Maybe it will help get me a place in Heaven when my time comes." She and her son waved good-bye as they continued on their trek.

Her unexpected kindness reminded me of a nagging moment when I was not so kind. It was on an Acela train from Penn Station to Boston. A young man in thick eyeglasses, dressed proudly in a too-large Boston Red Sox jacket, perhaps with limited mental ability, boarded the train with me and sat directly across from me. He smiled at everyone and let us know that he was traveling to Boston for the very first time by train. Every time the conductor walked through our car, the young man would stop the conductor to ask how much further.

When we got to Westwood, MA—Route 128, he must have decided that he was hungry and needed a snack and went to the café car. I thought it was a little late to be getting a snack since we were only minutes away from South Street Station, but minded my own business. Maybe he was really, really hungry. Just then the conductor called out that the Boston–Back Bay stop was coming up. The young man jumped up and began to gulp down his hot dog and soft drink, trying to keep his balance as the train sped over the tracks. He swallowed the last bite just as the train pulled into the station, brought down his duffle bag from overhead, and started to move to the nearest exist. I wondered if this were the correct stop for him, but didn't say a word. Nor did anyone else.

Until at the last second, a woman suddenly stood up, crossed over her seat mate, and ran after him. "If you want the Boston South Station, the main station, you don't want to get off here," she said kindly. He thanked her profusely at her unexpected act of kindness and sat down, red-faced from embarrassment of almost missing his stop.

But it was me that hung my head in shame. Why didn't I say anything? Why did I decide to mind my own business, when he clearly needed a little extra assistance? The incident still haunts me today (clearly since I am confessing it to all of you here now), and I am reminded of my own moment of unkind inaction by the unexpected act of kindness of that young mother helping me with my laundry cart.

Plato is attributed with encouraging us to "be kind, everyone you meet is fighting a hard battle." Perhaps I will need to do two acts of kindness a day for the rest of my life as penitence for the conscious and sometimes unconscious acts of kindness *not* taken for strangers as well as friends who are fighting their own hard battles. Maybe, just maybe, I might then be able to get a place in Heaven when my time comes.

· · · · · · · · · · · ·

"Heaven and earth are threads from one loom."

—Shaker proverb

Detergent, Mouthwash, and a Place to Lay One's Head

While in New York City recently, I woke up early, threw on some clothes and a jacket, slid a ten-dollar bill in my back pocket, and headed out to get a coffee, a croissant, a banana, and a yogurt. Ten dollars doesn't go far in the Big Apple, but I was pretty sure I had enough to make these few purchases.

Only a block away from my destination, a gentleman stopped me.

"Ma'am," he said. "I don't want any money." He quickly went on to explain, "I just moved into low-income housing and I start a new job tomorrow. I wonder if you could get me some detergent to wash my clothes and mouthwash for my breath? That's all I need. I don't need your money."

Looking into his eyes, I believed him but I only had ten dollars in my pocket and I was on my own mission to get some breakfast. Besides, maybe it was a scam; one can never tell.

I would like to tell you that I gave him my ten dollars or that I went into the drugstore to purchase those items for him. But I did not. And his very simple ask has haunted me ever since.

"Got a dollar?" I heard repeatedly as I walked the streets of Manhattan. Whatever happened to "spare change?" which I used to hear? Today, it's a dollar. But that gentleman didn't ask for money; he asked for detergent and mouthwash. Simple things that we all take for granted, but meant so much to him.

Portions of this essay first appeared as "Nowhere to Lay Her Head," in *Seeking God Day By Day* (Cincinnati, OH: Forward Movement, 2013). Used with permission.

It took me back to one morning while living in Cambridge when I awakened early to be at the laundromat when it first opened. The doors automatically unlocked at 7:00 a.m. and locked at 10:00 p.m. Imagine my surprise to find a young woman already in there. She called out a cheery hello, and I responded with a good morning.

And then I noticed. She was busily organizing numerous shopping bags around her grocery cart. I must have caught her as she was just washing up in the community sink. After layering a skirt over her slacks and a sweatshirt over her blouse, she then sat down to eat an apple for her breakfast.

I was impressed that she had found a safe, warm place to sleep that night. As 8:00 a.m. approached—when the dry cleaners opened on the adjoining side with the internal entryway—she hastily left the laundromat, with shopping cart in tow.

I sometimes forget that Jesus was homeless. He lived in community, relying on the hospitality of others for food and sheltering, owning little more than the clothes on his back and the sandals on his feet. If he were alive today, I am certain that Jesus would be found living and walking among the many invisible and often ignored faces of the homeless—the mentally ill, the physically disabled, the victims of domestic violence, the veterans, those with HIV, the young runaways, the families with children, the unemployed.

And he would have purchased the detergent and the mouthwash for that man. Mea culpa.

. . . .

"Foxes have holes, and birds of the air have nests, but the Son of Man has nowhere to lay his head."

—Matthew 8:20 (NIV)

The Risk to Love

Every morning I would see him outside the entrance to the subway, at the corner of Remsen and Court streets in Brooklyn Heights, New York. He would stare straight ahead with hands outstretched, mumbling under his breath, "Spare change." Never a question, always a declarative.

Everything he owned, he carried with him. He looked like a dirty, unkempt Santa Claus with his satchels trailing behind him. Often, he could be observed mumbling to himself, shaking his head in confusion.

Lent had begun, and I had promised God that every day I would do one act of kindness. So, on that particular morning, I reached into my change bowl in my apartment and dumped the contents into a baggie. My purse was heavier with its extra burden. As I approached the beggar, I reached into my purse . . . and then I hesitated. Keeping my head down, I walked by quickly, ran down the stairs, and moved toward the turnstile.

My action confused me. Why hadn't I given him the change? Later that day, returning home in an end-of-day rainstorm, I puzzled over my behavior. Then I saw him, standing outside the subway entrance to catch the commuters going home. I reached into my purse just as he began to walk away, huddling against the rain without umbrella or hat. He wasn't going to make me chase him, was he? Oh yes, he was!

Umbrella turned inside out, I ran against the rain as I struggled up the block. I finally caught up with him on Montague Street, just as he was entering a coffee shop.

"Here," I said, thrusting the bag of change into his hand.

He seemed as surprised as I was. I didn't wait for a thank you, too embarrassed by my own behavior. Continuing on to the grocery store, I felt better. After all, I was keeping to my Lenten discipline, wasn't I?

Or at least I thought I was, until I saw the same beggar on my way to work that following Monday. "Spare change," he called out to the passersby. I walked quickly past him, ducking my head. On the subway, I felt the shame come over me. I wasn't really keeping a Lenten discipline now, was I? Or had I just made some great pretense, some grand gesture? Oh sure, I had given him my spare change last Friday. But this Monday was a different story. What was I trying to prove, and to whom?

The next morning, as I approached him at the subway entrance, I braced myself. I tried to force myself to make eye contact with him, to say good morning. Nothing. On Wednesday, I spat out a good morning, as I walked quickly past him. He looked at me confused. Apparently, few ever wished him a good morning. On Thursday, I took a deep breath, looked him dead in the eye, and said, "Good morning." This time, he smiled.

On Friday, I approached him with a smile and greeted him with, "Good morning!"

"Good morning," he replied.

I handed him a quarter. "Thank you," he called after me, as I headed down the stairwell.

It then became our little routine. I would see him and he would wave hello. Our dialogue was simple: "Good morning. Good morning. Thank you." And, for a few moments, we connected as two human beings from heart to heart.

I learned a lot from that beggar that year because I realized that it is much too easy for me to think I have demonstrated my faith by one seemingly selfless act—such as giving the beggar all of my spare change on one particular day. But to begin to offer a genuine hello to that beggar every morning reminded me that it isn't so much about the gift as it is about the giving. And that it is not so much about the act as it is about the intention within my heart.

I often wondered whatever happened to that beggar. By the end of Lent, he was no longer at his usual spot. He reminds me of the bronze sculpture of the "Homeless Jesus" by Timothy Schmalz which depicts Jesus as a homeless person stretched out on a park bench. While his face and hands are covered by the blanket, the crucifixion wounds on his feet reveal his identity. The question of "What would Jesus do?" becomes then, "What if that was Jesus?"

May your Lenten practice this year allow space for you to draw nearer to God and search for the Holy through loving-kindness.

. . . .

"And the time came when the risk to remain tight in a bud was more painful than the risk it took to blossom."

—Anaïs Nin

The Simplicity of Choice

At 11:30 p.m. on Ash Wednesday on February 25, 2009, my friend Sandi wrote in response to her "never-ending, peace-robbing, forever-exhausting" struggle of seeking God's will for her life:

> "What if I simply CHOOSE to accept that I AM walking in God's will?
> What if I simply CHOOSE to accept—beyond a shadow of doubt—that I
> AM exactly where God wants me to be?
> What if I CHOOSE to REALLY believe that I have God's favor, and that He
> IS directing my path?
> Wouldn't this fundamentally transform my life?
> Wouldn't this allow me to really rest and enjoy my life?
> Wouldn't this give me peace?
> Wouldn't this give me power?!!!!
> In Jeremiah 29:11 (MSG) God says to me:

> > 'I know what I'm doing. I have it all planned out—plans to take care of you, not abandon you, plans to give you the future you hope for. When you call on Me, when you come and pray to Me, I'll listen. When you come looking for Me, you'll find Me.'

Portions of this essay first appeared as "The Simplicity of Choice," in *Finding God Day By Day* (Cincinnati, OH: Forward Movement, 2010). Used with permission.

For Lent (and hopefully beyond), I PURPOSE IN MY HEART not to second guess these things, but to SIMPLY accept these things as absolute truth."

—Sandi Haynes

She entitled that: "The Simplicity of Choice."

Now that is what I call radical faith. What if, on this day, I could accept that I am walking in God's will and simply choose to accept—beyond a shadow of doubt—that I am exactly where God wants me to be?

For forty days, could I choose to really believe that we have God's favor and that He is directing my path?

Jesus, full of the Holy Spirit, was led to the desert where he fasted, prayed, and resisted temptation. What would happen if I simply choose to accept that I am walking—like Jesus—in God's will for forty days?

The Simplicity of Choice. In response to my "never-ending, peace-robbing, forever-exhausting" struggle of seeking God's will for my life.

If You've Lost, Give Up

One of my responsibilities as an elementary school teacher was playground duty. Rain, snow, sunny, cloudy, cold, humid, it didn't matter. If it was my turn for playground duty, then off I went with the second and third grade classes for their twenty-minute break. On one such occasion, I came across the class bully who had his poor hapless victim on the ground as he relentlessly pummeled the child, demanding that milk money be relinquished.

As I ran over to rescue this latest victim, I could hear the smaller boy—clearly overmatched in both height and strength—shouting to his attacker, while at the same time trying to protect his face and his lunch money, "Do you give up? Do you give up yet?"

I eventually was able to break up the fight, and to this day admire that little scrapper who, despite his treacherous circumstances, refused to surrender. Mind you, he was sent home with torn jeans, a dirty t-shirt, scraped arms, and a black eye, but he didn't give up and—thanks to my intervention—he still had his lunch money.

Years later, I thought about him when, as a young professional, I was relaying to my great uncle about some stalled project of mine that seemed to get outmaneuvered time and time again by a cast of characters at work. I desperately needed advice from this revered sage on how to proceed.

He carefully listened to me as I went on and on about the false starts, mixed signals, and disappointing twists and turns. Finally spent, I waited to hear what he had to say. While I wiped away my tears and blew my nose, and as he waited for the kettle on the stove to heat up for his nightly cup of tea, he began to relay a story about one of his older sisters, my Great Aunt Gladys.

It seems that one day Aunt Gladys was walking down a busy street in Chicago, when some thug ran up beside her and grabbed her pocketbook (which was what purses were called back then) while the straps still hung over her arm. Rather than let go, she held on tight and was dragged halfway down the block before she finally was forced to let go. Aunt Gladys ended up in the hospital with a broken arm, a banged-up face, a dislocated shoulder, and no pocketbook.

"What does this have to do with my situation at work?" I asked impatiently.

"Well," he replied dryly as he turned off the burner under the kettle and poured the boiling water over his Lipton tea bag in his mug, "If you've lost, give up."

Because there just comes a time when one needs to move on. Or, as I finally learned: if you've lost, give up. Otherwise, you'll be like my Aunt Gladys or that third grader of long ago—remembered more for your foibles than for your feats.

Lot's wife, when fleeing Sodom with her husband and daughters, turned into a pillar of salt because she dared to look back, despite the warning from the Angels to only look ahead (Genesis 19). So be warned: new pillars of salt may be awaiting you, folks, if you insist on looking back.

. . . .

"You can spend minutes, hours, days, weeks or even months over-analyzing a situation; trying to put the pieces together, justifying what could've been, would've happened . . . or you can just leave the pieces on the floor and move the (expletive) on."

—Tupac Shakur

4

The Arc of Justice

The New Underground Railroad

H ave a nice day," the Latina sales clerk said as she handed me a very large cup of coffee with a big smile.

I had ordered and paid for a small coffee, but she intentionally had given me an extra-large coffee. It was only two days after the 2016 presidential election, and I—still reeling from the results—was walking around pretty much in a daze, uncertain how I should feel and even more frightening, whom I could trust.

But over the next few days and then weeks, I noticed a newfound underground of camaraderie, a renewed sense from people of color that we needed to—yes, we'd better—look out for one another. In department stores, grocery stores, airport, hotels, you name it, people of color seemed to be going out of their way to help each other. With a slight nod of the head and a quick shuttering of the eye, we were telling each other that it was going to be all right. We'd be watching out for one another.

It was reminiscent of the mid-1950s when, even as a child, I sensed there was this kind of twentieth-century underground, different from Cora's journey in the early 1800s as described in Colson Whitehead's *The Underground Railroad*. When we crossed the Mason–Dixon line in our tan sedan, we were well prepared, thanks to *The Negro Motorist Green Book*. There were certain ways that we needed to behave and only certain places where we could expect to receive any service. Mom always had a potty in the trunk of the car, and she brought along bologna and mayonnaise on white bread sandwiches wrapped in wax paper with a jug of water so that we did not have to stop to use public facilities or to buy snacks. Daddy knew which gasoline stations he could go to, and I even recall arriving at someone's house late one evening to spend the night. Apparently, calls had been made ahead of time that the Reverend and his family from up north needed a place to lay their heads on their way down south to visit his mother.

One Christmas, we rode the Southern Railway down to Atlanta. My sister and I, thinking it to be quite an adventure, did not understand the significance of our being seated in the segregated Pullman car where there were no luggage racks and the "colored" bathroom was so much smaller. I do remember that one of the porters took pity on two little girls who really had to go, and snuck my sister and me into one of the "white" bathrooms where we relieved ourselves in the sink. He kept shushing us to be quiet as he lifted us up (I giggling at the escapade and my sister distressed because she did not want to get her panties wet), anxiously looking back over his shoulder to make sure we were not caught.

It was the Jim Crow era. It was a time when, if we were walking down the sidewalk with our father in his hometown and a white man approached us, our father would gently move us off the sidewalk onto the street, tipping his hat, carefully avoiding any eye contact, and saying respectfully, "Yes, sir." It all seemed so strange and mysterious through my seven-year-old eyes. What I remember most—and what is again strangely familiar to me today—is the unspoken uniting of the "colored" people to make sure that we survived and were kept out of harm's way.

I understand that there is a restored Pullman Palace passenger car in the Museum of African American History and Culture as part of its inaugural exhibition, "Defending Freedom, Defining Freedom: Era of Segregation 1876–1968." It would be worth seeing, not only to remember that trip but also to never forget that Lady Justice, though blindfolded with her sword in one hand and her scales in her other, is not always so "colored-blind."

Two quotes seem right as I conclude this reflection. The first, inscribed on Dr. Martin Luther King Jr.'s memorial, was inspired by the nineteenth-century abolitionist Thomas Perkins and quoted by King often: "We shall overcome because the arc of the moral universe is long, but it bends towards justice." Or as Richard Pryor once joked: "You go down there looking for justice; that's what you find: just us." I thank God for this new twenty-first-century underground. I have a feeling that we are going to need it.

. . . .

"Justice: the maintenance or administration of what is just especially by the impartial adjustment of conflicting claims or the assignment of merited rewards or punishments."

—Merriam-Webster, 2018 Word of the Year

Staring Down the Bull

One news headline read, " 'Mother of All Bombs' Killed 94 ISIS Fighters, Afghan Official Says." Another headline reported that "Syria's Assad Says His Forces Not Dented by U.S. Strikes." Still another headline shouted, "North Korea Probably Can't Strike the U.S. Yet—But It's Still Plenty Scary."

Yes, it is . . . very . . . plenty . . . scary.

It reminds me of a time when I was at Union Station in Boston, waiting for my train back to NYC. A young man asked if he could sit at the empty seat at my table. I nodded yes, hardly looking up from my book.

Out of the corner of my eye, I noticed that he was of olive complexion, with a beard and dark pools for eyes. He brought out a tin, opened it, and took out a nail file. Suspiciously, I watched him file his nails and began to wonder if it could be a weapon. I noticed that there were small sheets of what looked to be sandpaper in the tin box, and he took out various ones to sand his nails.

My heart began to beat fast. A terrorist among us!? He asked gently where I was going. New York City, I replied. He then told me that he was going only twenty minutes away. He was a guitar teacher. And then I noticed that it was a guitar case by his feet. He opened it, brought out his guitar, and began to play.

I have since learned that guitar players prefer to have rounded or sliced-to-an-angle nails, with the shorter part toward the heart. Players often use different nail shapes according to their level of playing or the repertoire they are playing. It is thought that the only file suitable for the

Portions of this essay first appeared as "Sticking with Love," in *Seeking God Day By Day* (Cincinnati, OH: Forward Movement, 2013). Used with permission.

shaping of a guitarist's nails is a "Diamond Dust" file. After rough shaping with a diamond file, the nails are then sanded with 600 Grit Silicon Carbide paper. And that was what my table companion was calmly doing on that day—filing his nails as he waited patiently for his train.

That young man was strumming his guitar thinking only of peace and love. And on that day in Boston, I was thinking of war, drones, and terrorist attacks. Sadly, I do not believe that I would be any less apprehensive today than I was back then. News headlines of missiles, MOABs, and nuclear weapons do strange things to the mind. Indeed, I am probably even *more* apprehensive today because it's all really pretty doggone scary.

The next time I am in New York City, I must go visit the bronze statue of the Fearless Girl. Sculpted by Kristen Visbal and commissioned by the firm State Street Global Advisors in recognition of International Women's Day, it now boldly stands only a few feet away from the iconic bronze "Charging Bull" (which had enjoyed a solo act for the past twenty-seven years until the sudden appearance of Fearless Girl). There at the foot of Broadway near Wall Street, one little girl with a ponytail, chin up and hands planted firmly on her hips, has taken on the 11-foot, 7,100-pound "Charging Bull." On March 7, 2017, she took her position without fanfare in the dead of the night, planning to stay only a week, but due to the overwhelmingly positive response, the mayor has extended her permit to be there for another year.

A year is not a lot of time. It may take me at least that long to begin to muster up enough courage to begin to stare down those "Charging News Headlines." But if Fearless Girl isn't going to back down, then neither am I.

. . . .

"I refuse to accept the view that mankind is so tragically bound to the starless midnight of racism and war that the bright daybreak of peace and brotherhood can never become a reality . . . I believe that unarmed truth and unconditional love will have the final word."
—Martin Luther King Jr.

Truth, Lies, and Consequences

When I was in the second grade, our family eagerly awaited the arrival of the newest addition to our family. Every day my teacher would ask me, in front of the entire class, if my mother had given birth yet. One day, I got tired of the teacher asking, so I just said yes, it was a boy, and his name was Wesley Matthews Jr.

I lied. No baby had come yet, but we all just knew that it would be a boy and that my father would soon get his long-awaited namesake.

As luck would have it, my parents were waiting for me after school that same day, and my mother—as big as a house in her maternity top—waddled out of the car to go into the school. I pushed and pushed on her stomach, sobbing and crying, begging her not to go in. Of course, she did anyway and found out about my fib. A week later, my baby sister was born. Embarrassed, I suffered endlessly from the teasing—not only from my schoolmates but also my family—and was anointed with the nickname "Pinocchio." This sheer humiliation alone cured me of fabricating truths.

Around the same time as the arrival of my little sister, I "lifted" a package of what I thought was Chiclets (do you remember that classic brand of candy-coated chewing gum made by Cadbury Adams?) from the grocery store. I hid away in my bedroom and chewed the entire packet up in the same day, only to be found out because I had not taken chewing gum. I had stolen Feen-a-mint, which is a laxative. To add insult to injury, the next day my parents made me go back to the store to pay the sales clerk my nickel from my piggy bank for the stolen item and apologize for stealing—with all of the adults barely able to keep from laughing out loud at my misery.

In *Get the Truth: Former CIA Officers Teach You How to Persuade Anyone to Tell All* by former CIA officers Philip Houston, Michael Floyd, Susan Carnicero, and Peter Romary, readers are taught how to get the truth out of anyone without using torture. The authors give three reasons people lie. Either they: 1) fear the negative consequences of disclosing the truth; 2) want others to believe something about them that isn't true; or 3) want to avoid hurting someone's feelings. Further, the authors suggest that there are five behaviors that would indicate people are lying: evasion (failure to answer the question); persuasion (attempt to convince); manipulation (failure to understand the question); aggression (attack your credibility); and reaction (spike in anxiety).

My parents were not former CIA officers but they sure could have written that book! Perhaps it was because I was so inept as a thief or perhaps it was because of my parents' sheer intimidation ("let me look in your eyes, I can see that blue streak in your eye which means you are lying"), but all I know is that I got caught both times at a very young age. And there were consequences.

Alternative facts, half-truths, walking back, and "air quotes" . . . new words, phrases, and gestures in my lexicon. All I've got to say is that everyone should have had parents like mine who made me memorize the Ten Commandments and recite them daily for a month after my exploits, with #5, #8, #9, and #10 particularly ingrained in my soul. Seems to me, the world would be a much better place if we not only remembered but also practiced the Ten Commandments. What was good enough for Moses is good enough for me, and certainly should be good enough for the world today.

．．．．．．．．．．．．

"Whoever is careless with the truth in small matters cannot be trusted with important matters."

—Albert Einstein

When Pigs Fly

In May, we observe National Teacher Appreciation Week. As a child, I always wanted to be a teacher, so much so that the quote under my senior class picture in the yearbook was, "Go ye therefore, and teach all nations (Matthew 28:19 [KJV])."

In elementary school, my favorite teacher was my fourth-grade teacher, Mrs. Allen, who wore red high heels, pencil skirts, and had perfectly coiffed hair. She also found ways to challenge me and pushed me to learn even more. My favorite teacher of all was my high school geography and history teacher, Mr. Walburn. Geography and history weren't my favorite—or best—subjects, nor do I remember much of what I learned. I do remember Mr. Walburn's influence on my life.

You see, in the eleventh grade, I took the twenty-minute Kuder test, an assessment to help students identify career plans and "uncover amazing insights into their personal interests, skills, and values." Apparently, my extraordinary ambidextrous ability resulted in a very high score for a particular variable—chalk that up to being born left-handed but forced to change over to my right hand in the second grade. (Spending hours in after-school programs to learn to write with my nondominant hand is probably why my second-grade teacher is not among my favorites.) Based on my test results, my guidance counselor recommended that I become a secretary and consider attending a nearby black state college to receive my training in a two-year program.

I had other plans for my future, however, and they did not include becoming a secretary. I belonged to Future Teachers of America. I was going to teach school. A secretary, this was my future? Neither of my parents thought I should become a secretary. They too had dreams for my future—indeed, for all three of their daughters' futures—and that included a college education and becoming a professional. (Although my mother wisely told me that I had better learn how to type because I could always get a job as a secretary, which proved to be true during a couple of dry spells.)

After class one day, Mr. Walburn stopped me to inquire why I seemed so sad. I told him about my guidance counselor's recommendation.

"What do you care what that guidance counselor said?" he asked me. "Why, I was told that I should become a *pig* farmer. If I had listened to my guidance counselor, I'd be on a farm, slopping pigs somewhere, not here in this classroom teaching you."

A pig farmer?! Being told to become a secretary didn't sound half as bad as being told to become a pig farmer.

In *Being Disciples: Essentials of the Christian Life*, Rowan Williams, the former Archbishop of Canterbury, wrote: "Hope, like faith, is hope in relation; relation to that which does not go away and abandon, relation to a reality that knows and sees and holds who we are and have been. You have an identity not because you have invented one, or because you have a little hard core of selfhood that is unchanged, but because you have a witness of who you are."*

My eleventh-grade social studies teacher was my witness at a time that the choice of a different path could have irreparably changed my future. Thank you, Mr. Walburn, for being my angel walking the earth: for offering me hope, for being my witness of who I am. You changed the course of my life.

And thank you to all teachers who are making an extraordinary difference in the life of their students.

· · · · · · · · · · · ·

"Teaching kids to count is fine, but teaching them what counts is best."

—Bob Talbert

---

*Rowan Williams, *Being Disciples: Essentials of the Christian Life* (Grand Rapids, MI: Wm. B. Eerdmans, 2016), 29.

You People

I was in the third grade, and my mother had decided that my older sister and I could walk the five blocks to Highland Elementary School in Springfield, Ohio, only accompanied by our faithful dog named "Buppy" (my younger sister's botched attempt at pronouncing puppy). Buppy would escort us to school and then run home to let my Mom know that we had safely arrived at our destination.

Dressed in our freshly starched and ironed dresses, polished oxford shoes, ribbons in hair, and lunch boxes packed with a PB&J sandwich, hard-boiled egg (with salt wrapped up in wax paper), an apple, and a nickel for milk, we were ready for school. All we had to do was walk one block down West Southern Avenue to South Plum Street, made a right turn, walk up one more block to West John Lytle Avenue, turn left, and walk the three last blocks to our school.

An easy five blocks, or one would think. But it was the late 1950s, not too long after *Brown v. Board of Education*, and my parents had decided that their children would integrate the white elementary school rather than have us "cross the tracks" in the other direction to attend the all-black elementary school.

At the corner of West Southern Avenue and South Plum Street was Algo's, the neighborhood grocery store. As my sister and I turned the corner, a young white boy, dressed in a striped t-shirt with tan slacks, pulled his little sister by the hand off the sidewalk to stand with their backs to us on the grass, both facing the side of the store.

"We'll just wait until THEY walk by," he loudly told his sister, holding tightly to her hand.

My sister and I shrugged our shoulders, and with Buppy leading the way, continued our walk to school, swinging our lunch boxes beside us.

Later that day, as our mother prepared our after-school snack, I told her about the little boy and girl, and wondered what he meant.

Studiously pouring our glasses of milk and placing cookies on small plates, she finally said with pursed lips, "Pay them no mind. You just keep on walking to school and ignore them."

Fast forward twenty-plus years later, when I learned from my faculty advisor that, in defending my doctoral dissertation, one of my two outside readers had refused to approve my thesis until I rewrote my five-page abstract. Rewrite an abstract?! After three years of toil and sweat, a professor was standing between me and my hard-earned doctorate for a rewritten abstract?

Seated across from my great uncle in his apartment, as I relayed to him what had happened, I found myself once again crying and blowing my nose, looking to him for advice.

"You want the doctorate?" he asked. "Then rewrite the damn abstract and *apologize*!" he told me.

Apologize!!! Apologize for what? Didn't matter, he told me. Just apologize. So, I spent the night rewriting the abstract and attaching a handwritten note, asking for forgiveness for "any inconvenience" I might have caused the professor.

First thing the next morning, I placed the revised typed abstract in the professor's folder outside of the secretary's office in Judd Hall and walked across the street to the Reynolds Club to get a cup of coffee. As I sat commiserating with my fellow grad students, the professor walked in not five minutes later and saw me. He came over immediately.

"I read your abstract. It was much, much better," he said, nodding his head in approval. I breathed a sigh of relief. Finally, I would be Dr. Matthews.

"And what are you going to do now?" he inquired.

I proudly reported that I had begun a postdoctoral fellowship at Northwestern University to continue my research on the participation of women and minorities in math and science. He seemed shocked.

Clearly vexed, he began to shout, "That's what's wrong with YOU PEOPLE. . . ."

To this day, I cannot tell you what else he said. As I watched his lips moving, all I kept thinking was that in order to get my doctorate I had to apologize to him for being one of YOU PEOPLE. I apologized for being black, for being a woman, for daring to think I could earn a doctorate from the University of Chicago, for daring to think that I could become an educational researcher, and later for daring to go on to work for a community foundation, and then daring to become a managing director on Wall Street, for daring to be . . . ME.

My parents told me early on that the first thing that I must do is to forget that I am black; and the second thing that I must do is *never* to forget that I am black. Charlottesville, Boston, and Phoenix are yet again jarring reminders that, even today, I am still considered to be one of YOU PEOPLE; and yes, there are still those who will intentionally turn their backs on me, waiting for me to walk by so that America can be "great" again.

But the difference today? I refuse to apologize, and yes, indeed, just as my mother told me those many years ago, I'm gonna keep on walking.

. . . .

"Ain't gonna let nobody turn me around,
Turn me around, turn me around.
Ain't gonna let nobody turn me around,
I'm gonna keep on walking, keep on talking,
Marching up to Freedom's Land."
—Freedom Riders, 1961

Coulda, Woulda, Shoulda

It was September 26, 1990, and I suddenly found myself in a firestorm. A mayoral appointee to the Board of Education of the City of New York, I was being asked to vote on then Chancellor Fernandez's SAFE Program, a mandatory sex education class for middle and high schoolers that would include the distribution of prophylactic devices upon the request of students without parental knowledge or consent. We were a seven-member board, and somehow I had become the swing vote. Persuaded by the compelling statistics of AIDS and the growing prevalence of sexually transmitted diseases among adolescents, I voted yes.

I tried to stay out of the crosshairs of the press, even turning down an invitation from Oprah to be on her show. I was an educator. I had accepted the mayoral appointment to be about the business of education, or so I naïvely thought. How wrong I was.

Not unlike what we see today throughout our nation, New York City was all about partisan politics, and Rudolph Giuliani and his board allies were using any and every divisive issue to garner support for what ultimately would be a successful run for mayor. I received death threats; my mail was screened; my phone was tapped; and my car was followed.

Behind closed doors, the discussion became more and more vitriolic. The "Mooch" has nothing on my fellow board members. I remember one board member referring to the children in the New York City Public School system as "those dirty, little b@$#&ds!"

"And you can write that down, Westina," he said with pointed finger.

Portions of this essay first appeared as "Coulda' Woulda' Shoulda'," Letter to the Editor, Episcopal Café (August 11, 2017). Used with permission.

"Oh, I write down everything YOU say," I replied . . . because it was true. (If I ever wrote an article or a book about my public service experience, it would be entitled *That's Why the Children Can't Read*).

After months of heated debates, demonstrations, and unending media coverage, in February 1991 there was yet still another vote on a measure to allow parents to "opt" their children out from this program. On the evening of the board meeting, after noting how many people had signed up to speak to the board members on the upcoming vote, I lamented to a reporter, "Wouldn't it be wonderful if two-hundred-seventy-seven people were here to discuss an educational agenda?"

I knew how I was going to vote, and I was convicted. As the time to vote drew near, the then president of the board (also a mayoral appointee) beckoned me out of the room and told me that the mayor was on the phone.

I folded. I voted against my values. I voted politics over principles. It's a vote that I regret to this day. I should have resigned my position on the spot. I could have gone ahead and voted for the parental opt out. Knowing what I know now, I would have done it differently. Three months after that vote, I submitted my resignation to the mayor and did not fulfill my four-year term.

That vote almost cost me my life. Diagnosed with pericarditis (an inflammation of the sac around the heart), I am convinced that I nearly died from a broken heart of voting against my principles. A tough lesson to learn, but a lesson that I have taken to heart—literally—and have become known for taking maverick positions on principle while serving on subsequent boards.

On October 24, 2014, after a contentious and controversial trustee vote at an Episcopal seminary, the Rt. Rev. Andrew M.L. Dietsche, Bishop of the Diocese of New York, demonstrated courage and leadership in a letter, calling for repentance to all involved. He wrote, "Everyone has made mistakes, and every mistake has been compounded. My own failures or missed opportunities lie very heavy on my heart this weekend. And I am sorry."

Oh, how I wish I had issued such a statement after my vote those many years ago. Twenty-six years later, my own failures or missed opportunities still weigh heavy on my heart. And I am so very sorry.

Coulda . . . woulda . . . shoulda.

I so admire the late senator from Arizona who, at the time, was fighting an aggressive form of brain cancer and voted his principles over politics. Whether we supported or did not support his thumbs down, I hope we can all agree that he stood by his convictions. In doing so, he showed us that indeed, "a sling of truth still can make Goliath fall" as Tom Althouse once wrote in *The Frowny Face Cow*.

I wonder, is it only after we are forced to reach out and touch our own mortality that we are finally able to stand up for our principles? Is it only then that we can become a "profile in courage" and rise above all the politics, lobbying, and bullying?

In this Humpty Dumpty world, do any of us continue to believe in speaking truth to power? I ask because I don't know about you, but I sure do think that we need some new "heroes" and "she-roes" to serve as our role models on how to help put this world back together again. May I be so bold as to suggest that we consider beginning with an esteemed octogenarian senator who was not afraid to use his thumb like a sling?

. . . .

"A man does what he must—in spite of personal consequences, in spite of obstacles and dangers, and pressures and that is the basis of all human morality."

—John F. Kennedy

How Should I Think about This?

It was the first Saturday of May in 2011, and I was sitting out with friends on their back porch, discussing current events and catching up. One friend had just told us that this very question had been asked by her eleven-year-old daughter, after learning that Osama Bin Laden had been assassinated. Only a year old when the four coordinated suicide attacks by al-Qaeda occurred, this young girl had grown up in New York City, living in the shadows of the terrorist attack on the World Trade Center. I marveled that such a young voice could offer such a profound question: "How should I think about this?"

It is a question that I have been asking myself over these past seventeen years as well. Because on September 11, I found myself running down thirty-three flights in the World Financial Center and over the Brooklyn Bridge, running for my life with the two towers billowing with fire and smoke behind me. All I had with me were the clothes on my back, my purse, and prayer. As the first of the two towers began to collapse, I was fleeing—leaping over people who were tripping and falling in the sheer terror and confusion of it all. Not daring to look back, I just kept running; the smoke, the ashes, the debris fast approaching from behind, as if chasing me across the bridge.

Months later as I was leaving my parish located not far from the World Trade Center, after stopping to light a candle and pray for God to help me to forgive, I saw the (now famous) twenty-foot cross made of two steel beams jutting up from the enclosed fence. I knew then from

Portions of this essay first appeared as "How Should I Think about This?," in *Sacred Journey: The Journal of Fellowship in Prayer* 62, no. 3 (Summer 2011). Used with permission.

deep within my soul that I needed to begin the process of forgiveness and reconciliation, and wondered: "How should I think about this?"

Each year, we are further away from the terrorist attack, but each year there are new tragedies to mourn, and it becomes increasingly difficult, if not impossible, to ever forget. While the actual terror of that moment on 9/11 is becoming a more distant memory for me personally, I know that lives and jobs were lost, buildings destroyed, and our country will never be the same. Through God's grace, my heart has softened and my fear has been replaced by love.

The year 2011 was also the twentieth anniversary of Nelson Mandela's release from the Victor Verster Prison in Paarl (February 11). On several occasions while in South Africa, I have had the opportunity to visit Robben Island and to see the conditions under which he had to live. I wondered then (and still wonder) how President Mandela and Bishop Tutu were able to embrace this concept of peace and reconciliation, especially given the horrendous conditions of apartheid. I am convinced that they too must have grappled with the question, "How should I think about this?" and concluded that we can learn from them. I am ashamed by my own temptations to harden my heart over perceived or real injustices, large or small.

Also in 2011, I was in Burundi, a country in central Africa that had only recently ended twelve years of civil war (with President Nelson Mandela serving as one of the mediators). This civil war left behind many orphans, widows, HIV-infected people, and street children; and the church has become a place of comfort, love, peace, and reconciliation. I had an opportunity to spend time with Burundians who were also asking "How should I think about this?" One priest told me that he was almost killed five times, two of which were by his own ethnic tribe; yet, he pastors to everyone and preaches love and forgiveness. Another priest shared that his brother was poisoned by a neighbor at the age of two; his missionary father was killed when the priest was six years old; a sister was murdered; and another sister was mutilated. When I asked both priests if they were Hutu or Tutsi, they in turn asked me why it mattered. "We are one people, we must move on."

There is so much going on in the world that I find myself often still whispering that nagging question: How should I think about this? There is much to learn from others around the world who have begun to reconcile after conflict, whether it is in South Africa or in Burundi or closer to home. And there is still much to learn from the innocent question of an eleven-year-old who dared to ask: How should I think about this?

Each of us must learn how to live in the midst of broken promises, broken dreams, and broken relationships. We must learn how to forgive and how to move on with our own lives. Living in God's fullness of life cannot be done in the valley of resentment and unforgiveness. Transformation must come from within. So, how will YOU think about this . . . whatever *this* is for you on this day?

. . . .

"To love means loving the unlovable. To forgive means pardoning the unpardonable. Faith means believing the unbelievable. Hope means hoping when everything seems hopeless."

—G.K. Chesterton

A Return to Decency

With all the threats of wars, nuclear bomb testing, and provocative tweets, I wake up every morning to check the news first thing, afraid for what might have occurred during the night while I slept. Another shooting? Another terrorist attack? Another devastating natural disaster? Yet another explosive exchange of words between world leaders? I wake up, braced for what the day might bring. I fight fear every day, a fear of the unknown and the heretofore unthinkable.

This past year, I happened to be midtown in New York City on the day of the annual Veteran's Day Parade, which is the largest Veteran's Day parade in the United States. The parade had not begun yet, but the more than 40,000 participants were beginning to queue up at their assigned starting points, while bystanders began to congregate along Fifth Avenue.

At the intersection of 51st Street and Madison Avenue, the police stopped all traffic to allow a caravan of at least two hundred motorcycles to pass by, on their way to join the others for the parade. Engines were roaring loudly, and American flags were prominently displayed. Every rider had some symbol displayed to indicate that he or she was a veteran. People ran to the intersection, mobile phones in hand, to capture an image of the motorcade; and then almost spontaneously, applause erupted from the crowd with shouts of "thank you for your service" as the motorcycles passed by . . . and I was among them.

The following morning, on my way to church, over fifty uniformed Navy men and women, led by their commander, walked down Rector Street. Once again, spontaneous applause, accompanied by shouts of "thank you for your service" . . . including from me. They all smiled and nodded their heads, acknowledging our recognition.

What is this? In New York City—the cosmopolitan, global mecca of the free world—jaded New Yorkers spontaneously thanking our veterans!? Why, I hadn't seen anything like this in quite some time, perhaps since right after 9/11. I wondered aloud what the heck was going on with New Yorkers and with me.

I would expect such a response in Savannah, Georgia, home of Hunter Army Field Base, with the Marine Corps Recruit Depot on Parris Island, South Carolina, not too far away. On any one day in the Savannah airport, you might find soldiers in uniform departing or returning, with their families either tearfully saying goodbye or tearfully welcoming them back home. Indeed, it is not unusual to find oneself, on the short flight from Atlanta to Savannah, traveling with a cadre of fresh young Marine recruits—their eyes big as saucers filled with a strange mix of excitement and fear—on their way to boot camp. Often the airplane's captain can be heard on the loud speaker acknowledging the soldiers seated with us, thanking them for their service as they returned home. I've watched as a group of soldiers disembarked from their plane and passed by the gates to the exit, receiving standing ovations from the other passengers who were waiting to board.

But to see this in New York City? Even more perplexing, I was among those applauding and thanking veterans and the soldiers for their service! I who has never been too keen about singing "The Star-Spangled Banner," long before folks began "to take a knee."

Somewhere deep in my soul, I was touched with the awareness that these veterans and soldiers parading on this Veteran's Day had . . . and still do . . . keep me and this country safe. In sharing my observations with my sister (whose son retired after more than twenty years of service in the Air Force, including several tours of duty in Afghanistan), she observed, "I think we are clapping for them because they are reminding us what this country once was . . . and what we hope it will one day become again."

Could that be it? Were we clapping and thanking our veterans and military, hoping that through our vigorous demonstrations we could bring back a return to decency for our country? That we could join in a native call to bring a return to civil discourse?

Perhaps we found ourselves clapping and shouting, hoping that all of the hard-won battles for freedom, respect, dignity, and equal rights will not be lost forever. Perhaps it was our desperate plea and prayer that we will bring a return to decency . . . before there is so much damage that we will have forgotten what it means to be a patriot.

. . . .

". . . the true patriotism, the only rational patriotism, is loyalty to the Nation ALL the time, loyalty to the Government when it deserves it."

—Mark Twain

5

I Miss Who
I Was

Five Little Words

I am 97, not 98," she gently corrected me. "I was born in 1919."

I quickly did the math in my head, and realized my great aunt, who is like a mom to me, was correct. She and her husband had taken over the raising of me over forty years ago, allowing me to become a part of their loving, extended family. And yes, indeed, I had aged her by a year since her birthday five months ago. In this season of her life, every day counts.

Ten days before Christmas, I had flown into Indiana to spend a few days with her. We were seated in the living room of her small apartment in a seniors' independent living community—she on the couch with one cat curled up in her lap, the other cat nestled on the seat of her walker nearby, and I sitting in one of the two available chairs. A three-foot pre-lit, pre-decorated artificial tree stood on a table by her couch. Quietly we watched the snow fall outside her window, enjoying our time together.

"You know what I miss most?" she asked, breaking the silence.

Shaking my head slowly as I turned toward her, I was curious as to what she might say. Her house? Driving? Her husband? Clear vision? Mobility? Good health? Gourmet cooking? Which would it be?

"I miss who I was," she whispered.

There it was, the truth suspended in the air between us, as we oh-so-carefully and gingerly navigated crossing the tight rope of her life, hearts clinging to the balancing pole of the inevitable, with no net below to catch us should we fall. Five little words: she missed who she was.

This essay first appeared as "Five Little Words," in the *University of Dayton Magazine* (March 25, 2017). Used with permission.

I nodded, not sure what to say or even if I should say anything. The cat resting in her lap stretched lazily and purred; the other meowed in response. We continued to watch the snow falling on the tall pine trees outside of her window, two snow birds flitting in and out of the branches, as I waited to see if she would say more.

No other words followed. It would seem that she had said all that she needed to say in those five little words.

I miss who I was.

. . . .

"Spring passes and one remembers one's innocence. Summer passes and one remembers one's exuberance. Autumn passes and one remembers one's reverence. Winter passes and one remembers one's perseverance."

—Yoko Ono

Comfort

t's been a rough couple of weeks.

My newly turned 99-year-old great aunt called the police on her son because she was upset that he was leaving (after visiting for the past month to help take care of her). Weighing barely 110 pounds, a four-foot, ten-inch white woman asking the police to remove a six-foot black man from her premises in central Indiana . . . needless to say that did not go over too well. The texts and calls with family began at 11:00 p.m. and continued for several hours. That alone required a glass of wine.

After returning from a quick four-day trip to El Salvador where I co-led a workshop, my beloved and I landed at 10:00 p.m. only to be back at the airport at 10:30 a.m. the following morning to meet my daughter who was flying in from a business trip on the east coast. We turned around the next morning to go back to the airport to greet our son-in-law and two grandchildren who had taken a red-eye from the west coast to join us for the beginning of their family vacation. Out came the Klondike Bar.

Then my great aunt was rushed to the hospital for fluid around her lungs, and later we learned that she had suffered a mild heart attack. Because I have the healthcare proxy and power of attorney, I began juggling calls and texts with the case manager, doctors, nurses, and family, as we worked to have the doctor sign a "needs 24/7 care." Grabbed a Diet Coke.

All this was going on while two beautiful seven- and eight-year-olds were so-o-o glad to see Grandma and Grandad and spend time with us. Okay, then I reached for the glazed donut.

I finally got the family safely off to continue their vacation. The doctor signed the order. I interviewed two private-duty home care agencies over the phone, booked a flight to Indiana for later in the week, and convinced the hospital to keep my great aunt until Monday when care could be arranged at her home. At which point, I walked over to the kitchen counter and, spying the 6.6-ounce Pepperidge Farm Baked Goldfish snack crackers leftover from my granddaughters' visit, promptly sat down and consumed the entire bag (840 calories . . . I checked)!

Comfort foods.

Miriam-Webster defines comfort food as "food prepared in a traditional style having a usually nostalgic or sentimental appeal." We all have our comfort foods of choice. In my youth, it was mac and cheese. In grad school, it was Haagen-Daz pralines and cream—I would happily sit up on my bed with a pint of ice cream and a spoon, devouring the contents (this before I became lactose intolerant). As a young professional, a glass of wine and a bowl of microwaved popcorn always seemed to do the trick. Later, it was a turkey hot dog on a bun, lathered with mustard and relish, with a side of baked beans and potato salad. But I have been really, really good since moving down south, even avoiding the always available sweet tea and ordering my burger without the bun . . . that is, until these past two weeks.

I once heard a longtime recovering alcoholic share, "I'm really good at abstinence . . . alcohol, sex, food. It's moderation that I have a heck of a time with." No kidding, and I could see myself sliding down a slippery slope of no return.

Not to worry. I woke up Sunday morning with new resolve. After an hour-long walk and downing a protein shake, I practiced twenty minutes of qigong and a half of hour of yoga, followed by one hundred sit ups. I then hopped on my bike and pedaled to church. As I write this reflection, I am sipping on my freshly brewed ginger and green sugarless iced tea. I'm back in the saddle again.

Everyone deserves and needs comfort. I remember hearing a former CEO of a Fortune 50 company confess that, on 9/11, he went into his office, shut the door, and thought, "I want my Mommy." And then after the events of these past couple of weeks . . . well, I too wanted to go into a room, shut the door, and pine for my Mommy.

Yes, there comes a time when we each of us want our Mommy—whether the Mommy of the womb or the Mommy of the heart—and it is then that we might find ourselves reaching for something that helps to take us back to a time when life was so much more simpler and kinder. It's called comfort.

Thank God for wine, Klondike Bars, Diet Coke, Goldfish . . . and Mommies.

. . . .

"Some foods are so comforting, so nourishing of body and soul, that to eat them is to be home again after a long journey. To eat such a meal is to remember that, though the world is full of knives and storms, the body is built for kindness."

—Eli Brown, *Cinnamon and Gunpowder*

Lovebugs

Each year for four or five weeks, those black and orange insects called "lovebugs" (also known as the honeymoon fly or the kissing bug) are out in full force in the South. These lovebugs can number in the hundreds of thousands. They only appear twice a year—in late spring and again in September.

One day, two lovebugs landed on the windshield of our car on the passenger side where I was seated, right at my eye level, and they seemed to be holding onto each other for dear life. I have since learned that adult females live only three to four days, and the males live a little longer; and so, the adult pairs remain coupled, even in flight, for up to several days. When I told my beloved this, he responded, "Well, if I knew I was going to die, I'd be holding on for dear life too!"

When I visited my 99-year-old great aunt in early summer, during one of our after-dinner conversations, she told me that she was not afraid to die. She had carefully put her house in order—trust, healthcare proxy, power of attorney, investments. I was impressed and hoped that I would do as well when I reached her age. She was ready.

"The only thing I wish is that I don't die alone. I would like someone to be with me when it's time. I don't want someone to have to come in and find me," she shared wistfully.

I nodded, not sure what I could say to give her any reassurance that her wish would come true. She continues to refuse to move into assisted living, so she is still living alone. Thankfully, as a concession to

---

Portions of this essay first appeared as "Marveously Made," in *Abiding in God Day By Day* (Cincinnati, OH: Forward Movement, 2015). Used with permission.

her family, there was now a paid companion four hours a day, five days a week; on the weekends, she is all alone. (Although she has said, with a twinkle in her eye, that if I could find a good-looking young man to come tuck her in at night, she'd agree to that!)

Watching these lovebugs, holding onto each other for dear life, and thinking about my great aunt, I wonder: Who or what will be there for each of us when our time comes? Who or what will be our lovebug?

There are some nine hundred thousand different kinds of living insects, one and a half million species of animals, 422,000 known species of plant (and as many as 1,500,000 to 1,700,000 different scientific names are used to refer to them), and over seven billion people with 6,500 spoken languages in the world today. Yes, we are all fearfully and wonderfully made—including those lovebugs that are holding on for dear life—surrounded by God's love, hearing that sacred universal whisper of "you are loved."

. . . .

"Though lovers be lost, love shall not; And death shall have no dominion."

—Dylan Thomas

I Want to Be Ready

Are you ready?" I asked her as she collapsed in my arms. Her husband had just been wheeled down from surgery where a portacath had been inserted beneath the skin on his chest. We were standing in the hallway outside his room while four attendants carefully put his frail, thin body back into the hospital bed. I thought about this question of readiness over those next two weeks, as I made my daily trek to the hospital to sit with her, sit with him, or take her out for a meal while we waited for the inevitable.

I am faced with the question again, as I think about my great aunt with whom I visited the other week, making the twelve-hour door-to-door trip to check on her and see how she was doing.

"I'm sorry, I've never died before," my great aunt told me apologetically, as we sat at her table.

"Well, I haven't either, but we'll figure it out together," I reassured her.

I admire the maturity of my aunt as she prepares for her own inevitable. We have gone over all of her papers. I have patiently repeated the process for settling any outstanding credit card bills, arranging for the cremation and memorial service, and clearing out her apartment. What to do with the cats, Moonshine and Sunshine, her constant companions, is most on her mind.

Each night, she carefully picks out her pajamas, making sure they are clean and presentable should she die in her sleep.

Portions of this essay first appeared as "I Want to Be Ready," in *Seeking God Day By Day* (Cincinnati, OH: Forward Movement, 2013). Used with permission.

"I would like to not die alone," she confessed yet again. As much as I would like to promise that I will be there with her when her time comes, living 934 miles away, I cannot.

As we hug goodbye, she holds me tightly, whispering, "I hope I will be here when you come next."

I am startled by her statement. Looking her in her eyes I ask, "You sound as though you are ready. Are you?"

"No, not quite yet. But it just isn't any fun anymore."

This from a woman who drove around in a red convertible with the top down when she was my age. No, I don't imagine that this part is fun for her, as we awkwardly wait.

Are any of us ever really ready?

"I Want to Be Ready" is the title of one of the old spirituals. Each of us strive and desire to be ready. Like that song sung by slaves long ago, we want to be ready to walk into the "new" Jerusalem, wearing our long white robes.

God's love is placed in our hearts each Christmas, yet there is a season just before—the season of Advent—that asks us to awkwardly wait. Expectations have a lot to do with how we experience holy days, and the fruits of our waiting—hope, joy, love—are spiritual habits of the heart indeed worth cultivating.

And so today, just as I waited with my two dear friends in the hospital those years ago, I now wait with my great aunt, as we prepare for whatever is waiting for us just beyond the horizon. On the calendar, Halloween, Thanksgiving, Advent, Christmas, and then New Years are marked. Still, I will focus only on this day, and only hope that I am ready.

· · · · · · · · · · · ·

"If you get there before I do
Walk in Jerusalem just like John
Tell all my friends I'm a-coming too
Walk in Jerusalem just like John."
—*I Want to Be Ready*, Negro Spiritual

Kleenex, Toilet Paper, and Independence

"You know, there are so few things I can do for myself now," he shared. "I can reach for the Kleenex, reach for the cup of water, turn on the TV, reach for the urinal. Yet, they take that away from me. They put the stuff so it's easy for *them* to reach," he said disgustedly.

It was our first time alone since his surgery where they opened him up and just closed him back up again. Pancreatic cancer had ravaged his body. I was "uncle-sitting" as my great aunt took the weekend off.

"You know how Bets is. She starts fussing," he continued. "She moves the *TV Guide* over there, puts the flowers over here, puts the clock over there. Busy, busy, busy," he said with an understanding smile.

"Where do you want the things then?" I asked.

He arranged them exactly so, and I then left them there.

Over the weekend, we developed our routine. I would empty the urinal and then put it back on his left side, hooked to the first bar. The Kleenex box was at nine o'clock, the little alarm clock at high noon, the drinking glass at three o'clock—all resting on his bed stand that was to be positioned just above his knees. The remote control for the TV rested on the sheets on his right side. I never moved to get him anything unless he specifically asked.

As the days slowly passed, visitors would come and go. He would reach for something, and they would stare at me accusingly while they quickly intervened to do it for him. He would glance over at me with a slight smile and then graciously offer them a polite thank you. As soon as they would leave, I would reposition everything to where he wanted it.

Eventually, he stopped watching television, so it didn't matter where the remote was. He stopped wearing his glasses so he couldn't see the time on the clock. He was too weak to reach for the urinal, so I would hand it to him. But he still reached for the Kleenex himself.

Hourly, he would ask for the urinal. I would hand it to him, he would urinate and then hand the urinal back to me. Then he would reach for the Kleenex and wipe himself, and I would hold up the waste can for him to dispose of the soiled wipe.

The day before he died, he couldn't hold the urinal. I remember when his former boss and a former colleague visited that last afternoon. Requesting the urinal, I had started to help, but with indignant looks, the men dared me to assist. I watched these two grown men scurrying to help my great uncle, his penis no bigger than my baby finger. As had become his routine, he asked for a Kleenex to wipe himself.

I remember this because his wife—my now 99-year-old great aunt— is now in hospice care in her home. I have arranged for around-the-clock care, and family and friends are coming to visit. Like her husband from some thirty-two years prior, she too is creating her own routine, holding onto her own independence. Slowly and carefully moving her walker toward the bathroom, oxygen cord dragging behind her, she shakily sits down on the toilet seat and tears off the toilet paper to clean herself.

And just as her husband did those many years before, she too holds onto this last vestige of independence, folding the toilet paper carefully in her hands, sheet lined up perfectly with the prior sheet. And just as I did thirty-two years ago, I step back and wait, watching patiently . . . reverently . . . respectfully.

· · · · · · · · · · · ·

"Maybe this is what growing old was like, she thought. Maybe the world gets smaller and smaller until there's nothing but the walls around you to show you where you end and the rest of the world begins."

—Naomi Jackson

Until It's Time

"I just wish she would die," I sheepishly confessed to my priest after the Sunday morning service. Standing in the vestibule with head down, I shifted nervously from one foot to another, afraid to look up as I wiped away the tears from my leaky eyes. Seeking neither absolution nor reprimand, I just needed to hear myself say the words out loud, convinced my sin was beyond forgiveness. How dare I think such a thing, let alone say it aloud??!! If nothing else keeps me from entering those Pearly Gates, surely this will!

For ten long, what seems like interminable weeks, I have been overseeing the care of my great aunt who has been sent home from the hospital into hospice care. Managing all of the various moving parts—finances, hospice, round-the-clock aides, food, family, and friends—was exhausting. Doing it long distance was even a bigger strain. Would it be easier, I wondered, if I lived nearby? I think not. I think it would be even more stressful.

Of course, I didn't really *want* her to die. I will grieve deeply when she finally makes her transition. I just want it to be over. This waiting . . . and waiting . . . and waiting . . . was wearing me down. Ninety-nine years is a good long life, I think to myself; and I am certain that she does not want her own end of life to be on oxygen 24/7, unable to do much of her own personal care, heavily medicated to keep her comfortable, and with her short-term memory disappearing.

How do other caretakers do it? I wonder. I have new respect for family members who find themselves taking care of loved ones for weeks, months, or even years. How in the world do they do it? Who would want living their last days to be like my great aunt's? Certainly not me.

My sister and I continually remind her daughter (and my niece) that she will be the one who will be responsible for taking care of us when our time comes. We joke about it, but we are deadly serious, pun intended.

"I know, I know," my niece laughs. "And I already know that Mom will be the mean one, and you will be the nice one."

We laugh with her, but it's not really funny. We need reassurance that someone will be there to take care of us when it becomes our time. My sister keeps telling everyone, "Just put the drugs on the bed stand. I'll do the rest." I don't suggest the same, praying fervently that God's grace will be sufficient, and that I can be filled with radiant acquiescence for my own home-going.

I shared all of these dark thoughts with a dear friend who is a retired hospice nurse. Like the priest, she listened with a loving ear, without interruption or judgment.

"I guess it's a lot like childbirth," she shared. "In the throes of labor, you just want it to be over. But it's not, so you just have to labor on until it's time."

I once heard someone say, "I asked God to teach me patience, so He told me to wait." Now I just wait, praying fervently for patience while I labor on with my great aunt until it's her time. Until it's God's time.

. . . .

"Wait on the Lord: be of good courage, and he shall strengthen thine heart: wait, I say, on the Lord."

—Psalm 27:14 (KJV)

With This Ring

He was finally sober, after three previous unsuccessful stays in treatment centers. We were relieved. AA and Al-Anon had become our salvation, the life raft we clung to during those darkest days; then becoming our life support to remind us to breathe, take it a day at a time, and be filled with gratitude. We took nothing for granted and counted our blessings for every day of sobriety—which now was measured in months, not days nor weeks.

Somehow, in the midst of the worst of those drunken days, she lost her wedding band. She wasn't sure if it slipped off her finger or if she absentmindedly took it off somewhere, but it was gone. We searched high and low throughout their apartment—turning up cushions, emptying drawers, checking pockets, searching under furniture, examining contents of the vacuum bag and waste cans. No wedding band found.

It was strange to see her unadorned left hand entwined with the exceptionally long fingers of his right hand, as they looked adoringly into each other's eyes. Thirty years of marriage—through sickness and in health, for better or for worse—vows sealed by a gold wedding band that had somehow mysteriously disappeared.

It was early July, and her birthday was approaching. I had stopped by, planning to join them for dinner, as was my habit. As a struggling post-doctoral student, my annual stipend was stretched thin; and it was understood that I was always welcomed for a meal. She wasn't home yet.

"I need you to go down to the jeweler in Hyde Park and pick out a new wedding band for her," he said. "They know her ring size and I've already called. They are expecting you and they'll put it on my account."

Pick out a wedding band?! How will I know what to get her, I inquired? I hadn't really paid much attention to the missing wedding ring before it disappeared.

"You'll do better than I will," he responded. "You know that I'm not good at picking out gifts for her."

Which was true. How many times had I heard him tell her on many occasion, "Go on down and pick out something you want from me." The same request for Valentine's Day, their anniversary, Christmas, or her birthday; she would obediently make some coveted purchase to bring home and show him what he had bought for her. His eyes would twinkle, and he'd smile with glee that she had what she wanted. She would kiss him on the cheek, he would say "you're welcome," and both seemed content.

The next day, I dutifully dragged myself down to the jeweler, examined carefully the wide assortment of wedding rings, and finally selected a simple 18-carat-gold band. Finding her size, the jeweler placed the ring in a box, and wrapped it up prettily with a bow. I never asked the price, and immediately scurried over to the apartment to deliver the goods.

"Did you get it?" he whispered, as I handed him the package. A big grin spread across his face as he went into the bedroom to hide it away.

At her birthday dinner, he presented her with the gift. Tears filled her eyes, as she slipped the band on her finger. He and I smiled at one another, never sharing our secret until this day.

Last month, I found the wedding band tucked away in the back of her jewelry box. He has been deceased now some thirty-five years. I am not sure when she stopped wearing the ring, but I know he is not forgotten—a large full-color portrait of him is hung on the wall by her bed.

I slipped the ring on my finger on my left hand, next to my own wedding ring. It fit perfectly. I am still wearing her ring, finding comfort in remembering both the love they shared and the love they showered on me. Somehow, it makes this time of her own transition just a little easier to bear.

In sickness and in health, for better or for worse, until death do us part.

. . . .

"No couple buying wedding rings wants to be reminded that someday one of them will have to accept the other one's ring from a nurse or an undertaker."

—Anne Tyler

Waiting Faithfully

One of my favorite pictures of my great aunt is of her sitting on the couch in the sunroom of her former house, elbows on knees, hands tucked under her chin, as she smiled at the camera. Eyes twinkling with a tiny smile, she clearly was thoroughly enjoying life. It was taken when she was in her early eighties.

It would seem to be her favorite position, for I am now watching her in that very same position again; but this time on the couch in her small apartment. With few exceptions, she has slept on this couch since she came home from the hospital in late August, at her own insistence. For whatever reason, she does not wish to sleep in her bed. A sheet covers the cushions of the couch and blankets are folded at one end, pillows on the other. Tethered to the oxygen tank, weighing only about 100 pounds now, she sits with her hands under her chin, elbows resting on her knees, nasal cannula in her nostrils, staring into space. Not saying a word, just staring into space and waiting.

She observed earlier in the day that the way she knew she was old was by looking at her hands . . . hands with thin fingers gnarled and reddish-raw. She tries all kinds of creams on her hands but nothing really seems to give her relief. She has her nails polished by the caregiver; they are a bright pink today.

When I reminded her that she was 99 years old and that meant her hands were 99 years old, she cackled with glee, thinking that was the funniest thing she had ever heard of! Imagine that . . . she was 99! Why, she didn't know anyone in her family who had lived to be 99.

Dementia is increasing and we had a particularly difficult time the day before. No longer recognizing me, I am only Westina "her friend." Finally, at 10:00 p.m., wanting to leave the apartment and go to her "home," she buttoned up her coat, pulled up the collar, cocked a brimmed hat on her head, and asked me who she was pretending to be. Katharine Hepburn? Joan Crawford? I finally guessed correctly—Humphrey Bogart. We clicked our glasses—hers a scotch on the rocks and mine a glass of cabernet—as she congratulated me for finally figuring out who she was. I guess she wanted to be anyone besides a 99-year-old woman with gnarled hands and pink painted fingernails, on oxygen, waiting to die.

Now on this afternoon with the sun beginning to set, we sit in her apartment. I in a chair seated across from her, reading a book on my Kindle and sipping a cup of coffee. She with elbows on knees, hands tucked under her chin, looking out into space.

Thomas Merton once wrote that "Time is not given to us to keep a faith we once had but to acquire a faith we have now." And so, we rest in this time of faithfully waiting . . . and waiting . . . and waiting.

. . . .

"Here's looking at you kid."
        —Rick (played by Humphrey Bogart) in *Casablanca*

The Decision

I t's time, you know."

The silence hung between us across the miles, as if on an invisible clothesline. I sighed heavily. It was my niece Amy on the telephone. A vice president for a bank, she tended to be more business-like and factual. Like I used to be before I retired, before I became responsible for my great aunt in hospice care at home.

Amy was right. It was time to move my great aunt into a nursing home with memory care. Continuing to keep her at home was proving to be increasingly costly and unmanageable. I had so hoped that she would be able to transition in her own home, but it seemed not to be. As she told me when she first came home from the hospital in late August, waking me up at 1:30 in the morning, wheeling in on her walker with eyes wide open, "You tell Spirit, that I don't like The Plan. I am not following The Plan! Call him up and tell him right now!!!"

This past Saturday, she asked the live-in caregiver to take her to the store to purchase a new pink suitcase and pink lipstick because she needed to begin packing. She was going home. As one dear friend reminded, "Your aunt may be losing her memory but she has not lost her ego!" We keep the front door to her apartment locked so that she will not try to walk out in her night clothes.

The brochure provided by hospice indicates that when the loved one begins to talk about "going home" and seeing deceased family members, it is part of the "symbolic language" for end-of-life. My aunt has been going home for the past couple of months as the dementia continues to increase, and yet she is still here.

When the nursing home sent the head nurse to do the initial in-take assessment, we were afraid that she would pass the dementia test of thirty questions, having done so twice before, most recently in May. She was pretty clever with the nurse. When asked to write a sentence, she wrote between bites, "Next time please come after I have eaten," as she sat at her table finishing up her breakfast.

Once the thirty questions were completed and as she began to talk in her rambling way, it became clearer. She proudly shared that: she was from Loyola; she was now in Detroit being held in prison against her will; she was 65; she did all the cooking and cleaning herself; that woman by the stove (her caregiver) was her prison guard; and would the nurse (who my great aunt thought was a police officer) please go back to his office and have his boss come and arrest that woman and set my great aunt free so she could finally go home?

I already had prepared a list for when she made her final transition: legal, financial, obituary, memorial service, notifications. I had not prepared a list for moving into a nursing home. It's a different kind of list: labels for clothes and personal items; decisions on which furniture to take; need for a nursing home assessment and a doctor's order; legal documents required for me to assume full responsibility . . . the list goes on and on. (I did remember to request that her doctor put in the order that she could have one Dewar's on the rocks with a splash of water each night in the nursing home.)

Burying a child, or parent, or spouse, or loved one is never easy. For whatever reason, we seem to be a little more accepting of the inevitable if the person was very ill or very old. As a child and even into my mid-30s, I recall waking up in the middle of the night, hyper-ventilating, terrified of the thought of dying. After surviving two life-threatening illnesses and running for my life on 9/11, the fear has subsided, at least for now. Who knows? When my time comes, I may be like my great aunt, insisting that some relative call up Spirit and tell him that I don't like The Plan, either.

Perhaps that is why turning fifty is such a threshold for so many of us—we realize that we will most likely not live as long as we have lived, and different decisions and priorities begin to be made. Still, I think that few of us are ever ready to think about no longer walking this earth, even we who believe in eternal life.

I find some comfort in remembering how my great aunt at 85, standing in her kitchen in her then house, telling me very matter-of-factly, "When it's time and it becomes too much for the family, promise me that you will put me in a nursing home." I scoffed at such a thought back then. That was before . . . before it was actually time to make The Decision. Somehow, that memory comforts me, as I pray fervently that, even as she now looks through a glass dimly, I am doing what she would do if she could make The Decision herself.

We are not the first family to go through this, nor will we be the last. Yet, it doesn't make any of it easier. No, it's not very easy at all because it is time now to make The Decision.

. . . .

"She considers the past. She measures it and weighs it and holds it in her hand like a plum. The past is everything now, and she understands that this is what it means to be dying: You stop looking forward, instead living for moments that happened years before."
—Thomas Christopher Greene, *The Headmaster's Wife*

6

Stranger, Wanderer, or Friend

First You Need a Bowl

Marvene Sampson was an outstanding teacher's aide at the only public elementary school in the town where I taught. It was the early 1970s and Marvene, a Vietnam widow (her husband was shot down while flying a helicopter on a rescue mission), was single-handedly raising her two sons. Every now and then she would bring in a pan of her homemade rolls to school, and oh how we all loved them!

One year, I wanted to prepare a special Easter meal, and the menu included rolls. Not only did Marvene generously share the recipe, but she also sat with me in the teacher's aide room—among the smell of ditto paper, crayons, paste, and glue—as she demonstrated with clay on a linoleum cloth how to roll out the dough into small "snakes" and fold into roll shapes. Homemade rolls quickly became one of my signature offerings at meals and potlucks.

Many years later, after I had moved from Ohio and relocated to New York City, I remembered Marvene's homemade rolls. I had been invited to a "down home" southern potluck dinner in Manhattan, and I planned to surprise everyone with the rolls. I called Marvene one evening; we were both glad to hear the other's voice. It had been at least fifteen years since I had either spoken with or seen her. I explained that I wanted to use her recipe to make those delicious homemade rolls.

"Now remember, Marvene," I cautioned her, "I haven't made these rolls in over fifteen years. Start from scratch with the instructions. I'll call you back tomorrow at 8:00 p.m. for your recipe, please."

Portions of this essay first appeared as "First You Need a Bowl," in *Meeting God Day By Day* (Cincinnati, OH: Forward Movement, 2014). Used with permission.

The following evening, I called at the appointed hour.

"You ready?" she asked. "Do you have a pen and paper?"

"I'm ready," I replied, pen poised to write down the recipe on lined notebook paper.

"Well then," she began very slowly, "first you need a bowl . . ."

Dutifully and carefully I wrote down the instructions as she dictated them to me.

Marvene passed on to her glory in 1995, leaving behind her recipe for homemade rolls. At least twice a year, I now dust off that piece of notebook paper, yellowed and aged around the margins, stained with flour, mashed potatoes, and butter. And as I prepare to make the rolls, I begin to read those inspired words: "First you need a bowl. . . ."

. . . .

"Always start out with a larger pot than what you think you need."

—Julia Child

Marvene's Mashed Potato Rolls

(Makes 2 dozen)

Ingredients:

- ½ cup mashed potatoes (okay to use the packaged kind)
- ¼ cup butter
- ¼ cup sugar
- 1 teaspoon salt
- 1 cup scalded milk
- 1 package yeast "mothered" in ¼ cup warm water
- 4 cups unbleached flour

Directions:

1. In a large bowl, mix well with mixer: potatoes, butter, sugar, salt, milk, yeast, and 2 cups of flour.
2. Put in 2 more cups of flour, or enough to make a soft dough.
3. Form a ball.
4. Cover inside of bowl with oil.
5. Pat dough in bowl, and turn it over.
6. Cover with wrap; let rest an hour.
7. Or you can put ¼ cup of oil in bag, put in refrigerator at least 2 hours.

    This will keep for up to 2 days in the refrigerator. If you put in refrigerator overnight, it will need to be punched down in the morning.
8. Make up rolls, let rise again (about 1 hour).
9. Preheat oven to 400°F.
10. Bake until golden brown, brush tops with butter.

Friendships

Having just returned from four days in New York City and then two days in Raleigh, I realize that I have always traveled a lot . . . for jobs . . . for family and friends . . . for vacations. When I lived in the Midwest, I actually looked forward to the hour-long shuttle van ride to and from the airport because I would meet the most interesting people and hear the most fascinating stories.

On one such ride, I met a woman who was a public relations director for hotels. She had the longest fake eyelashes—upper and lower—I had ever seen; it was all I could do not to ask her how she put them on. In less than an hour, I knew that she was originally from Baton Rouge, into her second marriage, temporarily unemployed, and off to her hometown for a visit. From the depths of her purse, she pulled out a wallet crammed with photos (this was before iPhones and social media) of her and Andy Griffith in California, her and Kenny Rogers' brother in Missouri, and her and Henry Kissinger in Illinois. As she exited the shuttle van, she turned and said, "Oh, by the way, my name is Mary. What's yours?"

I discussed this phenomenon of strangers sharing their lives so openly during brief encounters with a sociologist friend of mine. He noted that there is a theory that everyone can be classified at one time or another as a friend, a wanderer, or a stranger. As the theory goes, upon the initial meeting, you are first a stranger with the potential to become a wanderer or a friend. It is with the stranger that "true confessions" are shared.

Portions of this essay first appeared as "Choosing Friends," in *Meeting God Day By Day* (Cincinnati, OH: Forward Movement, 2014). Used with permission.

We mused aloud why it is that some words stop conversations and others seem to carry the conversation further along. I recalled striking up a conversation with a fun-loving group of women on the van to the hotel while on vacation years ago and learning that they too were from Brooklyn. We were laughing and having a great conversation, but when they heard me say that I was from "Brooklyn Heights" (in response to their question of what part of Brooklyn was I from), all further conversation ceased.

Curiously, there are certain words that seem to introduce an uninvited intimacy that we may not be prepared—or desire—to share. Whatever that word, known only in hindsight—this sudden forced intimacy can feel as though strangers instantly know too much about us . . . certainly more than we ever intended for them to know.

I am not convinced that any response to questions about where I went to grad school or college—or even where I live—are genuinely *about me*. What do you really want to know, I want to ask. The movie I just saw and enjoyed? My favorite music? What I am reading? Or perhaps even my dreams and hopes? Instead, with only a word or two, the conversation ends—abruptly and without any explanation. It's safer simply to say "Brooklyn" rather than "Brooklyn Heights" and let the conversation continue along.

So back to stranger, wanderer, or friend.

The British anthropologist Robin Dunbar suggests that we can really only maintain five close friendships at a time. (Tell that to Mark Zuckerberg.) Continuing my meandering thoughts with a clergy friend over tea, she wisely suggested that sometimes when one friend begins to enlarge his or her own world, the other might begin to think how small their world seems in comparison and, in turn, begin to withdraw even more. Or sometimes the friend may be the kind of individual who is open to new possibilities—always seeking to stretch and grow—and views the friendship as an opportunity to continue to expand his or her horizons. Perhaps that's what keeps it down to five close friendships?

I suppose it's a little like a few items in my closet that are still with me after thirty-plus years. Yes, over time fashions change and even my own style has changed. But look in my closet and you will find: a beautiful black Harvé Benard sweater with an appliqué of leaves and berries on the right shoulder bought in Michigan City, Indiana eons ago; a black wool shawl that I picked up in Salzburg on an August afternoon when the temperature dropped unexpectedly; a lightweight washable purple fleece coat from Woodstock; and a green, loose silhouette cotton sweatshirt from Oberlin College. Each has been a consistent mainstay in my wardrobe . . . for better or for worse, in sickness and in health, for richer or for poorer, and through thick and thin.

Just like those clothes that have been with me for decades, I count among my friends-for-life: a sister from birth, a friend from high school, two dear friends from college, three friends whom I met in the first months I began to work on Wall Street, a sister of a former boyfriend (glad he's gone, even more glad that she stuck around), and three friends from my years of living in New York City. I can think of three or four newer friends who look like they will be with me for a lifetime as well. I have a wide circle of sister-girlfriends and brother-man-friends, and treasure those too. But friends-for-life, not so many.

I handle each of these friendships with special care: paying attention to mend when anything is torn, and to treasure the precious gift of unconditional love and acceptance offered. We share and celebrate one another's personal triumphs and victories, as we move purposefully from being a sister or brother "in your face" into living in God's good grace. Like my old and familiar wardrobe, each of these friends has been with me . . . for better for worse, in sickness and in health, for richer or poorer, through thick and thin . . . from Yellow Springs to Menlo Park to Chicago to New York City to along the Wilmington River.

. . . .

"When we honestly ask ourselves which person in our lives means the most to us, we often find that it is those who, instead of giving advice, solutions, or cures, have chosen rather to share our pain and touch our wounds with a warm and tender hand. The friend who can be silent with us in a moment of despair or confusion, who can stay with us in an hour of grief and bereavement, who can tolerate not knowing, not curing, not healing and face with us the reality of our powerlessness, that is a friend who cares."

—Henri Nouwen

Somebody's Mama's Recipe

We first gathered in 1999, ten professional women who were baby boomers, and each of whom were within arm's reach of either side of 50. Intentionally diverse, the only requirement seemed to be to be earnestly searching for how to transition into this new uncharted territory in our lives. At our first gathering, most only knew one or two of those in our group.

Over these past nineteen years, two members have dropped out for various reasons, but two others magically and seamlessly were invited into the group. At the time, we all lived and worked in Brooklyn or Manhattan, but now one is in Chicago and I am in Savannah. We meet at least quarterly, usually at someone's home during a weekday—although we've been known to meet at a Chinese restaurant to celebrate Chinese New Year or find a weekend to head upstate New York for a "girls weekend" away.

It's potluck—breaking bread seems to be one of our traditions. Crowded around a dinner table by candlelight—passing food and wine—we each take turns sharing our fears, our triumphs, our frailties, and our challenges. There is no judgment, just tender listening and open arms; and yes, sometimes the wiping of tears.

We have discussed unwelcomed body changes that come with growing older as well as suspicious lumps in the breast; solemnly observed the birthdays of three of our members when they found themselves older than their own mothers when they had died; survived 9/11; celebrated first-time grandchildren; and sorted out if and how much longer we wanted to work full time, whether or not to go to graduate school to retool, and how to manage being members of the sandwich generation. Over the years, jobs have been lost and found, new careers have begun, cleaning ladies shared, graduate degrees earned, physicians referred, books published, loved ones buried, and friendships deepened. We continually support one another outside of our gathering through emails, texts, phone calls, and personal visits—sick beds, graduations, weddings, holidays, and funerals are all observed and shared. It is a sisterhood formed out of love but not of blood.

Our closing for each gathering is the same. Having carefully listened to each other, we all join hands. One prays for the woman on her right, lifting up in prayer the joys and concerns that were shared during the evening. A gentle squeeze to the woman to her right and the prayer circle continues until we are back to our beginning—an endless and timeless circle of loving women friends.

It was a hot and muggy August evening in the backyard at one of our gatherings. We were sitting under a canopy and snuggled tight around a table, breaking bread together. Madeleine, our hostess, had made corn on the cob rolled in butter and parmesan cheese. It was her mother's recipe, she said. Jackie had brought a wonderful coconut cake for dessert, and we all exclaimed how delicious it was.

When we asked Jackie where she got her recipe, she replied, "I don't know. It's somebody's Mama's recipe."

We all howled as we shared our favorite "somebody's Mama's recipe," our mouths salivating as one favorite recipe was shared (in great detail, I might add) after another.

Sisterhood . . . lifelong friendships formed around the table, breaking bread, sipping wine, and eating "somebody's Mama's recipe."

. . . .

"I would rather walk with a friend in the dark, than alone in the light."

—Helen Keller

Jackie's Friend June's Old Kentucky Home Coconut Cake

- 3 sticks unsalted butter
- 2 cups sugar
- 5 extra-large eggs
- 1½ teaspoons vanilla
- 1½ teaspoons almond extract
- 3 cups all-purpose flour
- 1 teaspoon baking powder
- ½ teaspoon salt
- 1 cup whole milk
- 4 ounces sweetened coconut (Baker's)

For the frosting:

- 1 pound cream cheese (Philadelphia)
- 2 sticks unsalted butter
- ¾ teaspoon vanilla
- ¼ teaspoon almond extract
- between ½ to 1 pound (regular size box) confectioners' sugar
- 6 ounces sweetened coconut (Baker's)

Directions for the cake:

1. Preheat the oven to 350°F.
2. Grease two 9-inch round cake pans.
3. Dust lightly with flour.
4. Use electric mixer to cream the butter and sugar until light and fluffy.
5. Add the five eggs, one at a time, while mixing.
6. Add vanilla and almond extracts and mix well.
7. In a separate bowl or over a sheet of wax paper, sift together the flour, baking powder, baking soda, and salt.
8. With mixer on low, add the dry ingredients and the milk to the batter, alternating dry ingredients with the milk. Mix until just combined.
9. Gently fold in the coconut.

10. Pour batter evenly into pans.
11. Bake 45 to 55 minutes or until toothpick comes out clean.
12. Cool on a baking rack for 30 minutes.
13. Then turn the cakes out of the pans to complete cooling.

Directions for the frosting:

1. Use electric mixer to cream the cream cheese, butter, vanilla, and almond extract on low speed.
2. Add the confectioners' sugar to taste (you'll use between ½ and the whole box), and mix until thick and smooth.
3. Frost the cake.
4. Sprinkle the top with coconut and lightly press coconut onto the sides.

Healed in the Presence
of a Child

The second Sunday of June is traditionally Children's Day. As a child, I always looked forward to the observation of Children's Day at our church. It was a Sunday when music was provided by the Children's Choir, children read the scriptures and served as the ushers, and the seminarian delivered the sermon. It was also a time to recite a poem or scripture during Sunday school. The parishioners were warm and supportive, offering encouraging smiles and applauding our efforts. It was a Sunday when we children felt very, very special.

I thought about Children's Day when I was part of a small tour group led by Ahmed "Kathy" Kathrada at the Liliesleaf Farm in northern Johannesburg, South Africa. This farm was the center of the liberation movement, and served as the secret convening place during the early 1960s. It was the evidence found on this farm that led to the famous Rivonia Trial and convicted Kathy with his other comrades—including Nelson Mandela—to twenty-six years as political prisoners, eighteen of those on Robben Island.

Kathy shared with the tour group how he would stand on a stool in his cell at Robben Island and look over to Capetown located only 5.5 miles away, longing to be able to walk freely in nature to enjoy flowering gardens, indigenous trees, and wade in the choppy water. The rest of the group moved on to hear more about the truck on display that had been used to transport arms from across the border that were hidden under a false floor.

Portions of this essay first appeared as "In the Beginning," in *Abiding in God Day By Day* (Cincinnati, OH: Forward Movement, 2015). Used with permission.

Mesmerized by the reminiscing of this wise and humble man, I stayed behind. Kathy turned to me and lamented, "No one has asked me what I missed most." Answering his own question, he responded, "Children . . . the laughter of a child, the crying of a child, the singing of a child. I did not see a child for twenty years; and when I finally did, I began to cry."

Fyodor Dostoevsky once wrote that "The soul is healed by being with children." I believe that Ahmed "Kathy" Kathrada's soul was healed in the presence of a child.

Once back in the United States, strolling freely in the gardens and parks while watching children play happily with one another, I wondered how many of us take for granted being able to see children; and to this day I am still filled with boundless gratitude for Kathy's unintentional reminder of why it is so important for us to observe Children's Day.

. . . .

"Your children are the greatest gift God will give to you, and their souls the heaviest responsibility He will place in your hands."

—Lisa Wingate

Let Them Eat Cake

I met Jennifer while in graduate school at the University of Chicago. We lived in the same student housing building. An art history major, Jennifer took me to my first art museum, The Chicago Art Institute, and introduced me to the world of art. Understanding that I was a total novice when it came to art appreciation, she wisely suggested that the Impressionists were probably the place to start for me, and how right she was!

My personal tour guide, Jennifer colorfully shared the back stories for the masterpieces by some of the world's most beloved artists, including: Manet, Degas, Monet, Renoir, Cézanne, Cassatt, Gauguin, van Gogh, and Toulouse-Lautrec. A lively and intelligent student with a quick wit, she made art fun, interesting, and accessible.

And at least once a week, I was in her apartment, eating something made out of her Crock-Pot or from her oven. A southerner, she knew a lot about comfort food; and as graduate students, we needed a lot of comfort!

One day, she called me up to have dessert. "I've made lemon pound cake," she proclaimed. "Come up and take a break from your studies."

One bite into her cake, still warm from the oven, and it made me want to "jump up and smack yo' mama," as the old folks used to say (an old southern expression used to describe smackin' good food). Moist, tart, and sweet—the cake melted in my mouth. I begged for the recipe, fearful that either she wouldn't give it to me or that it would be impossible to replicate.

"It's easy," she said. "You can do it. It's a one-step pound cake where everything goes into one pan. All you need are a Bundt pan, flour, sugar, lemon yogurt, lemon, eggs, and a tub (one cup) of Parkay margarine."

Yes, a tub of Parkay margarine. (Some of us might remember those Parkay commercials where a talking tub would say "butter" to a character who would mention Parkay. Trust me, it is not butter.) Highly processed, this margarine includes a lot of things that are probably not good for you, but it sure does make a good cake.

Over the years, I have made this no-fail lemon pound cake—using the same Bundt pan that I purchased with scarce extra money available back then as a graduate student. Always using the same pan, and always with a tub of Parkay margarine. I have no idea if any other kind of margarine or butter works; I have never tried.

"Let them eat cake" is the traditional translation of the French phrase "Qu'ils mangent de la brioche," which can be found in Jean-Jacques Rousseau's autobiography *Confessions* (1765). Some 250 years later, I am still adhering to Rousseau's suggestion by making and eating this one particular cake.

Thank you, Jennifer, wherever you are, for introducing me not only to the world of art but also—and perhaps more importantly—how to make a one-step lemon pound cake. I guarantee you that this no-fail cake will make you want to "jump up and smack yo' mama!"

. . . .

"A party without cake is really just a meeting."

—Julia Child

Jennifer's One-Step Lemon Pound Cake

1. Grease and flour tube pan or large Bundt pan.
2. Have oven at 325–350°F.
3. In a large mixing bowl, combine:
   - 2¼ cups flour
   - 2 cups sugar
   - ½ teaspoon salt
   - 1 teaspoon baking soda
   - 1 teaspoon vanilla
   - 1 cup soft margarine (the kind in a tub)
   - 1 8-ounce carton lemon yogurt
   - 3 eggs
4. Bake 60–70 minutes until done.
5. Cool in pan 15 minutes, remove from pan, cool completely.
6. As it is cooling, glaze with confectioner's sugar mixed with lemon juice.

Broken Pieces

I have a dear friend named Bonnie. One summer evening I was standing with Bonnie at the subway stop. We were so involved in our conversation that we did not notice any one around us. Quietly, I heard a little boy whisper to his mother, "Look Mommy, that lady's leg is broke."

I did not give it much thought, until I realized that he was pointing to Bonnie.

You see, Bonnie has only one leg, having become an amputee at age five. Bonnie has pushed past the limitations of her disability. A Rhodes Scholar and Harvard graduate, Bonnie has a rich background that spans the gamut from sales at IBM and Wall Street to the White House National Economic Council to success as owner of her own motivational speaking, coaching, and writing business.

And so, here we were on a hot muggy July evening, Bonnie and I standing on the corner of Broadway and Wall Street in Manhattan dressed in sleeveless blouses and in sandals so that our arms and feet could breathe. We looked like most others walking along the street at twilight.

The only difference was that Bonnie's right leg is an artificial leg. The particular prosthetic she wore that evening is what she calls her "sports leg," and there were metals and screws for the leg part that ended with an artificial flesh-like foot with pink nail polish painted on the toes to match the toes on her left foot.

Portions of this essay first appeared as "Expectations and Imperfections," in *Finding God Day By Day* (Cincinnati, OH: Forward Movement, 2010). Used with permission.

I was not seeing Bonnie's prosthetic. I only saw this amazing, courageous, intelligent, *beautiful* woman who is a prayer warrior and a new dear friend.

Yet, that little boy saw a lady with a "broken leg."

My friends, aren't we—each of us—in our own particular way . . . broken? Aren't we . . . each of us . . . in our own special way . . . broken pieces?

On this day, I do not know what you think is broken. Is it a broken heart? Or a broken home? Or a broken marriage? Or a broken body? Or a broken job? Or a broken promise? Or a broken spirit?

Do you expect others to be divinely perfect? Do you expect yourself to be divinely perfect? God does not ask us to be perfect. God only asks you to be perfectly human.

And in that brokenness, let me share with you one of my favorite prayers: Father, forgive me for expecting in others that which I can only expect in the Divine.

. . . .

"Just as I am, without one plea,
But that Thy blood was shed for me,
And that Thou bid'st me come to Thee,
O Lamb of God, I come! I come!"

—William Batchelder Bradbury

Two Cents' Worth

I was six and she was five. We were best friends. We would walk to school together, meeting at the corner at our assigned time, escorted by my dog Buppy and her dog Sam.

We would laugh and trade sandwiches from our lunch boxes. I'd always have peanut butter and jelly; she'd always have baloney. Mine was wrapped in wax paper, hers in a paper napkin. We'd trade half sandwiches.

We would play together at recess, but because I was a grade ahead, we were not able to sit together at lunch. So, we'd sit at our grade-assigned tables in the cafeteria, wave at each other from our respective tables, and plan to meet on the playground later.

Milk cost a nickel. Sometimes my mom would give me a dime and let me keep the change. Sometimes her mom would give her a dime and let her keep the change. About twice a week, we'd find ourselves with a nickel to spend at Algo's, the neighborhood grocery store, on the way home from school.

Because we were such good friends, we'd split the nickel evenly, two cents for me and two cents for her. I'd buy licorice and she'd buy bubble gum. And then we'd throw the extra penny away. Ceremoniously, we'd stand over the street gutter and drop the extra penny through the grate. That's how good of friends we were.

But I was a year ahead of her in school, and I learned how to divide. One day, I figured out that if we saved the penny, we'd each have three cents the next time we had a nickel. I couldn't wait to tell her of my newfound knowledge.

We met outside the school doors. She showed me that she had five pennies this time. She felt very clever, because this time she had thought to ask the lady who collects the milk money for five pennies change.

We looked at the pennies and counted them out. She had held the extra penny out to me and said that I could do it this time.

I looked at her and I looked at the penny. She was my best friend, and she had figured out how to ask for five pennies change, all by herself. She trusted me and she liked me. She was willing to throw away her extra penny for me.

I took the penny and threw it as far as I could—which wasn't very far; it landed in the bushes nearby. We skipped down the street, hand in hand, with Buppy and Sam yapping at our heels, on our way to Algo's. I'd buy licorice and she'd buy bubble gum.

I was six and she was five. Next year, she'd learn how to divide, and then we could begin to save our pennies. But for right now, we'd just be even. We'd be best friends.

. . . .

"Piglet sidled up to Pooh from behind.
    'Pooh!' he whispered.
    'Yes, Piglet?'
    'Nothing,' said Piglet, taking Pooh's paw. 'I just wanted to be sure of you.'"

—A.A. Milne

7

The Thin Place

Not by Sight

We stood on the rooftop of our building at 6:50 p.m. on March 7, looking up at the sky for a sighting of the space shuttle *Discovery*. The shuttle's thirteenth and final visit to the orbital outpost—it had undocked from the International Space Station earlier in the day for the last time as it prepared to make its descent back to Earth. An hour earlier, my neighbor had excitingly told me that we would be able to see a very bright light in the sky if we looked north at about 6:54 p.m. Would I like to join her?

Arriving to the rooftop before my neighbor, I watched two small lights move quickly across the sky and had pointed the moving specks of light to her when she joined me. But she was convinced that what I saw was not it. "It's supposed to light up the entire sky," she insisted. Shivering in the 39-degree temperature (with a wind chill of 31°F), we kept looking for the bright light that we were told would "light up the sky." We could see the small white clouds of our breaths as we looked up during long periods of silence, craning our necks to catch a glimpse of a big, bright light shooting across the sky. Breaking the silence, my neighbor quietly said that she appreciated that someone in our building had imagination and would share the moment with her.

We saw a lot of airplanes flying overhead, but nothing that looked like the Space Shuttle. Finally chased inside by the wind and cold, we gave up, never seeing the space shuttle *Discovery* on its final mission. Sensing her disappointment, I reassured her, "Well, even though we didn't see it, it doesn't mean that it didn't happen." I knew beyond a

---

Portions of this essay first appeared as "Seen and Unseen," in *Seeking God Day By Day* (Cincinnati, OH: Forward Movement, 2013). Used with permission.

shadow of doubt that the STS-133 crew members were somewhere up in space, and that they were scheduled to land at 11:57 a.m. on March 9, 2011, at the Kennedy Space Center in Florida. Seen or not seen by us.

We learned the next day that we actually had seen the Space Shuttle. It had passed the Village of Suffern, New York, at 6:55 p.m., and was easily visible as two small stars moving in tandem across the sky. Is that not like our faith sometimes? We think that God will be revealed as a great burst of light that cannot be missed. But often instead, God moves quietly and determinedly toward that still quiet place within ourselves where love and peace reside; and if we can trust our inner voice that is whispering into our very being by our Creator, we will begin to discern the great mystery of each and every blessed moment. If we can only believe, seen or not seen, walking by faith and not by sight.

. . . .

"Now faith is the substance of things hoped for, the evidence of things not seen."

—Hebrews 11:1 (KJV)

God Rest 'Em

'm the kind of person who rarely cries publicly. When I do cry, I wait until I am at home alone; and when I feel the tears coming on, I go into the bathroom, close the bathroom door, turn out the lights, get into the shower, turn on the water full blast, and cry.

There seems to be some sort of shame that I attach to crying, or some kind of defect that I have because I'm supposed to be able to handle things. Everyone expects me to, including myself. And so, I cry in showers . . . alone.

There have been a few exceptions, though. I remember my senior year in college, the evening that I was crowned the first black homecoming queen at my university. Except I didn't know I had been elected queen yet. The relentless false accusations by the other candidates and their managers had finally gotten to me. So there in my dorm room, I sat and began to cry. The head resident came to my room, took one look at me, and called the Dean of Women, who came over to my room. Seeing that I was inconsolable, the Dean of Women called the Dean of Students, who arrived next. She took one look at me and called my parents who drove the thirty miles to the campus, and they joined the others in my room. And I sat in my dorm room sobbing. For two hours, I just sat there sobbing. A floor resident for the dorm, the students on my floor all gathered outside of my room, while I sat inside and cried. Finally, I dried my eyes and headed to the football field. I didn't care who was elected queen. I didn't even want to go. Not after they had all watched me cry.

Portions of this essay first appeared as "Everlasting Life," in *Finding God Day By Day* (Cincinnati, OH: Forward Movement, 2010). Used with permission.

I won, but to this day I am embarrassed to confess that my pictures from that historic evening are not among my best . . . puffy eyes, tear-streaked cheeks, and a drippy nose do not photograph well.

Seventeen years later, I cried at the Westwood Cemetery in Oberlin, Ohio, having just interned my great uncle's ashes on his mother's gravesite. As we prepared to leave, I started to cry. Sobs came up from my belly—long, deep sobs. I didn't have a tissue. I kept asking for a tissue. Wads were thrust into my hands, while I just kept crying. Later, no one mentioned my crying jag. I think crying for a loss of a loved one is somehow more permissible. It's a kind of sanctioned grief.

Perhaps because we just observed Holy Week and celebrated Easter, the news of death seems to be everywhere . . . a high school classmate, a friend's mother, another friend's father, yet another friend's brother-in-law. Some of us mourn privately, sharing our grief with a few, tucking memories close to our hearts. For others of us, we might find ourselves crying uncontrollably at the oddest times.

Mourning is a universal experience. I remember in May 2010, three days before the exhibition closed, I slipped into the Metropolitan Museum of Art to view "The Mourners: Medieval Tomb Sculptures from the Court of Burgundy." There I saw thirty-seven alabaster mourner figures—each about sixteen inches tall—created by the fifteenth-century sculptors Jean de la Huerta and Antoine Le Moiturier, taking over twenty-five years to complete, to honor the tomb of John the Fearless, the second Duke of Burgundy, and his wife, Margaret of Bavaria. The procession was led by the choir boy holding a candle, each statuette intricately carved to show such deeply personal and intense grief.

Whether at the burial ground for African slaves in Lower Manhattan; the Tomb of the Unknown Soldier in Arlington National Cemetery; the graves of the eleven murdered in the Jewish synagogue in Pittsburgh; the mass graves after the earthquake in Port-au-Prince, Haiti; the seventeen killed and buried in the massacre at Marjory Stoneman Douglas High School; the burials of the fatalities in Camp Fire in northern California; or Stephon Clark—an unarmed 22-year-old black father of two killed by a policeman in the backyard of his grandmother's home in Sacramento—there were mourners still inconsolable and filled with desolation.

We may not always be able to afford such a luxurious memorial as John the Fearless, yet the grieving may often be equally as deep and sometimes as long in duration. Statuettes or no statuettes, marked graves or unmarked graves, processions or no processions, tears or no tears.

. . . .

"Now is your time of grief, but I will see you again and you will rejoice, and no one will take away your joy."

—John 16:22 (NIV)

To Forget or to Be Forgotten?

was surprised to receive a call from her, a longtime family friend and one of my "aunties." I am always glad to hear from her. In her late eighties now, my recent experience has been that for her to remember where to find my telephone number, let alone to call me, was nearly impossible. Hence my surprise hearing from her and sounding like her old self.

"I'm calling to invite you to my daughter's wedding this weekend," she said animatedly. "I know it's late notice, but she really wants you to come. Are you in town?"

I sadly regretted, saying that I had an unavoidable conflict, privately knowing that her daughter had married over thirty years ago. Auntie was confused . . . again.

This auntie is confused a lot lately. Caretakers are with her around the clock in eight-hour shifts, which she vehemently resents. When I was with her recently for what I hoped would be a fun outing, it was clear that her short-term memory was almost non-existent. As we prepared to leave her apartment, her questions were non-stop: "Where are my keys? Where are we going again? Where is my purse? Where are my keys? When do we leave? Where is my purse? What time does it begin? Where are we going again?" I patiently and lovingly answered each of her questions, but could not help but feel concern.

According to the Alzheimer's Association, the number of Americans living with Alzheimer's disease is growing—and growing fast. An estimated 5.5 million Americans of all ages have Alzheimer's disease. One in ten people age 65 and older (ten percent) has Alzheimer's dementia, and almost two-thirds of Americans with Alzheimer's are women. The disease typically progresses slowly in three general stages—mild (early-stage), moderate (middle-stage), and severe (late-stage). Since Alzheimer's affects people in different ways, each person will experience symptoms—and progress through the Alzheimer's stages—differently. Or as one octogenarian pithily remarked about her own memory lapses: "First there's part-timers; then there's all timers; and then there's 'craft,' which stands for can't remember a [expletive] thing!"

Several years ago, when I first noticed mild indications of my auntie's loss of memory, I shared my concerns with her family who readily concurred. They took her to doctors for evaluations, but surprisingly she refused to be further tested or to receive any treatment. I later asked her why.

"I just don't want to know," she whispered. "I don't want to *know* if I am losing my mind. It frightens me."

Consequently, there was never a complete medical evaluation nor any medications prescribed to help ease her symptoms. We sadly watched her slip from mild, to moderate, to what I fear will soon be severe dementia. I take some comfort that she still remembers me and will call me on occasion. But how much longer will she know me?

I recall my then 97-year-old great aunt telling me that she "missed who she was" and wistfully lamenting not remembering as much as she used to. Names, places, and events have slipped by her, tucked away in some memory bank of long ago. Now when I gently ask her about some past event, she quietly reminds me that it was a long time ago, and she can't be expected to remember *everything*, which is absolutely true.

Still, sometimes my great aunt worries that she is beginning to remember less—from who stopped by to visit her the day before to which restaurant she went to over the weekend—and she seems to be equally frustrated that she must now use a walker. I asked her once which would be worse: to lose her memory or to have lack of mobility? She quickly responded that she'd rather have to use a walker than to lose her faculties.

Every sixty-six seconds someone in the United States develops this disease. (But let me hasten to reassure you, dear readers—and myself—that having occasional lapses in memory does not mean necessarily that you have Alzheimer's.) It might make one stop to wonder what it would be like to be unable to remember who you once were and therefore unable to even miss who you were. Or as Joyce Rachelle so poignantly posed in her question, "Is it more painful to forget, or to be forgotten?"

I'm not sure. But it's a question to ponder, with a promise to remember my auntie even when she cannot remember herself.

. . . .

" 'Pooh, promise you won't forget about me, ever. Not even when I'm a hundred.' Pooh thought for a little. 'How old shall I be then?' 'Ninety-nine.' Pooh nodded. 'I promise,' he said."

—A.A. Milne

Running Out of Time

Edwin C. "Bill" Berry entered my life by deliberate design. My maternal grandmother (whom we called Nana) was his oldest sister, and she decided that we should meet when I moved to Chicago to begin my doctoral studies. She flew in on a November day (impressive, since her daughter—my mother—never flew on a plane one day on this earth).

When I arrived on the doorstep of the Berry's luxurious co-op apartment, Nana swung open the door and said, "Finally!"

Finally? Hardly final. Perhaps a beginning. Bill and Betsy Berry took on the care and feeding of Westina Matthews. I am fond of saying that I was raised in Yellow Springs, Ohio, but I grew up in Chicago, Illinois. A poor, struggling graduate student, I wore socks on my hands for gloves, owned two pairs of blue jeans and a yellow ski jacket (the only coat that I owned) to keep me warm on those bitterly cold days in Chicago. The Berrys took me on as their next project with a loving, firm hand.

They took me to my first banquet at a hotel (in her borrowed clothes). Uncle Bill drove me to Johnson Products Company to get my hair relaxed and cut. Two jars, twenty-four inches less, and five hours later, I had "blow hair" that rested softly on my shoulders. Aunt Betsy would open up her closet and pass along her very fine hand-me-downs, and take me into her bathroom (his and her bathrooms, have you ever?) and show me how to apply makeup.

I remember coming home from a date and proudly announcing to Uncle Bill that I had eaten my first lobster. As he began to rub down hard on my arms and shoulders, I asked him what he was doing. "Rubbing some of the hick off of you," he said with a strange mixture of delight and disgust.

When did they become Mom and Papa instead of Aunt and Uncle? I'm not sure. Maybe it was the day that they introduced me as "one of their kids." They were always picking up various kids along the way, five altogether, who became my "brothers and sisters." But—Bill and Betsy declared emphatically—I would be the last one.

Having lost my own father, Wesley Matthews (after whom I had been named), at about the same time that I "lost" my first husband, I desperately needed a man in my life whom I could count on, believe in, and look up to. And Bill Berry fit the bill—pun intended.

He was a great civil rights leader, former head of the Chicago Urban League, television host, consummate fundraiser, and chairman of the committee to elect and reelect Harold Washington; mentor to many, peacemaker for others; articulate, tall, handsome, funny, smart, and wise. He was my Papa. We became practically inseparable. He was a tough and unrelenting teacher who often left me in tears. Until one day I asked him, "Don't you like me?"

He seemed startled by the question, and softly replied, "Don't you understand? I don't have a lot of time left. I finally have someone that I can leave all this with, and we don't have much time."

Not much time? An alert, agile man in seemingly good health. His only vice was chain-smoking, having given up alcohol a few years back. But he must have known something that I didn't know. That he was running out of time.

. . . .

"Yesterday is gone. Tomorrow has not yet come. We have only today. Let us begin."

—Mother Teresa

Between Two Worlds

Diagnosed with pancreatic cancer only four weeks prior, Papa (which is what I affectionately called my great uncle) was fading quickly. Confused and disoriented much of the time, he was visibly weaker and sleeping quite a bit. His liquids were restricted to only one ounce of ice chips per hour which he greedily sucked off my finger. A tall, lanky man when in good health, he now weighed less than one hundred pounds.

"Ken's here, Papa." I announced, concerned that he would be unable to recognize one of his favorite mentees who had come for his first and only visit to the hospital.

What an act of courage and love it required for Ken to visit his beloved mentor one last time. I watched these two men, who loved and respected each other so deeply, saying their final goodbyes. While tempted to leave the room to give them privacy, I felt drawn to stay.

"Did you bring Esther?" Papa asked in a surprisingly clear, strong voice.

I was taken aback, not only by the question but also by the clarity of the question. Only minutes before Ken's arrival, I had told Papa how I wished that I could understand him better when he was speaking, his voice raspy with his words barely audible. Now, here he was curled up on his hospital bed, asking Ken about someone named Esther.

"She's coming, you know," he stated matter-of-factly.

He then proceeded to invite the four of us—Ken, Papa, Esther, and me—out to dinner. And would it be okay if he brought along his own mother, Muzzy, he asked? Muzzy was here, too.

"I'll just take a nap for a few hours and then you two can come back later," he continued. "We'll all go out to dinner. And Wes, you get my money together because I want to take Muzzy along. My wallet is in the drawer here by my bed. Just the five of us, okay?"

Beckoning me outside of the hospital room, a visibly shaken Ken whispered to me that Esther was his mother's name, dead now some ten years. Suddenly weak in the knees, I found a seat in the waiting room. I wasn't sure whether to cry, to faint, or to just be. Inhaling a deep breath, I decided just to be. Don't think, I kept repeating to myself. Don't think. Just show up and be present. Don't try to rationalize and intellectualize this experience. Just accept that whatever was happening was really happening. My mind said it could not be so, but it didn't matter because my heart already knew.

Papa died the following day, May 13, 1987, on Muzzy's birthday. Deceased more than twenty years, his mother came back to help her son cross over. There is an old Celtic saying that heaven and earth are only three feet apart, but in the thin places, that distance is even smaller. It is a place where "we are jolted out of old ways of seeing the world," writes Eric Weiner. It is a place where the veil is lifted so that we might catch a glimpse—for just a brief moment—of what lies beyond the here and now. And in that one precious moment, I was privileged to be invited to witness someone straddling between two worlds, one foot in each, balancing on the spiritual edge of that thin place, surrounded by love.

• • • • • • • • • • • •

"Your mind cannot possibly understand God. Your heart already knows."

—Emmanuel

A Better Question

Well, that's not the best question to ask to get the answer you want," responded Dr. Quentin Young, a longtime family friend and physician.

We were having one of our daily long-distance phone conversations, consulting on the progress or lack of progress for my great uncle who had become like a father to me. I had just asked if the cancer was spreading.

"The simplest answer to your question is 'no,'" Dr. Young continued. "Now a better question would be, 'Is there any evidence to explain our problem?'"

There was something about his question that prompted a different response, a better answer. To his question, I received a more detailed discussion about the change in medication, the level of pain, the level of coherency, and the results of the latest tests. It would seem then to be all about asking a better question. Over the next three weeks, I asked this better question that prompted a better answer, until neither further questions nor answers were required.

Every second, Google receives over 54,000 queries; and on a daily basis about fifteen percent of all queries submitted have never been seen before by the Google search engine. In order for the algorithms to trigger the two hundred unique signals or "clues" that make it possible to guess what one is looking for, the broader and yet at the same time more precise the query, the increased possibility one can get the answer one is looking for. It is somewhat of a paradox: choose words carefully, use explicit phrases, but include as many words as might appear on a website.

I thought about this as my beloved, a devoted gardener, was searching on the internet to confirm the identity of a flowering plant that he was considering for our yard and also to figure out where it would be best to plant it. The initial question—"What kind of Camellia do I have?"— was a dead end. But asking "Where should I plant my Camellia?" took him to the website for the College of Agricultural & Environmental Sciences at the University of Georgia Extension where he was able to identify the order (Ericales), the family (Theaceae), the genus (Camellia), and the species (*japonica*, also known as the rose of winter).

I suppose it is what Jacob Getzels, a renowned educational researcher on creativity and intelligence, told us in a graduate class over forty years ago: "Your challenge is to ask the question that may have never been asked before. Search for the right question."

In other words, ask a better question to get the better answer.

Oh, in case you are interested, *Camellia japonica* typically blooms from January through March, is generally planted in the late fall through the early spring, and is shade loving. We will be planting our camellias initially on the southwest side of our house.

· · · · · · · · · · · ·

"To ask the 'right' question is far more important than to receive the answer. The solution of a problem lies in the understanding of the problem; the answer is not outside the problem, it is in the problem."

—Jiddu Krishnamurti, *The Flight of the Eagle*

Gubby's Shirt

"Go get Gubby's shirt," my mother would say to one of us girls. "Time to put on the shirt."

Gubby, formally known as George LeRoy Fields, was born on July 27, 1894, and died at the age of 59 of a heart attack while driving his car down a back road on July 26, 1954. He was my maternal grandfather whom we all called Gubby.

My mother loved her father dearly and there were only three things she kept of his: a pocket watch, his reading glasses, and the green striped cotton shirt that Gubby was wearing when he died. For weeks, my mother slept with that shirt, soaking it with her tears until she was able finally to put it away.

His shirt only came out when one of us was really, really sick. We didn't go to doctors routinely, relying on home remedies for almost everything. My mother would rub Vicks on our chest and throat, pin a dirty sock around our neck (I guess dirty because it was going to get pretty funky), place a sliced raw onion on a plate under the bed (supposedly when it turned black it meant the fever had broken), make us eat a finger full of Vicks (did you ever notice on the jar that it says NOT to take it by mouth?), and wrap us in Gubby's green-striped shirt. Tucked tightly into bed beneath sheets, blankets, and quilts, we stayed there until we sweated out the fever. To no one's surprise, we got better out of sheer self-defense.

When I was getting married to my first husband back in 1970, my mother cut off a small piece of Gubby's shirt no bigger than the palm of my hand, saying, "Here. You will need this."

My mother must have had a crystal ball because my little piece of shirt could be found attached to me by a safety pin whenever I became sick: head cold, flu, bronchitis, strep throat, pericarditis, you name it. If I got really, really sick, I not only pinned the shirt to me but also rubbed my chest and neck with Vicks, pinned a *clean* sock around my neck, and curled up with a heating pad. I passed on the onion, quilts, and eating Vicks. Somewhere over time, I began pinning the swatch of cloth to me during any time of great trials; just knowing it was close to me provided comfort.

After our mother died, as my sister and I were going through Mom's things, we came across Gubby's shirt, tattered from over forty-two years of use. Without hesitation, we quickly found a pair of scissors to divide the shirt into five larger pieces so that each member of the family would have a section. We mailed the others their piece of Gubby's shirt without note or explanation. None was needed.

My mother was very good about knowing what to give me to keep me going through the unforeseen tough times ahead. It was Fall 1977, and I was about to go off to graduate school in Chicago. Our family did not have a lot of money, but my mother wanted to give me something . . . some expression of love, hope, and faith. She gave me a gold-plated chain on which hung a small glass bulb containing a mustard seed presented in a small white box lined with cotton.

"Honey," she said. "I don't have much to give you, but I want you to have this. Remember, so long as you have the faith of a single grain of mustard seed, all things are possible, if you only believe."

The original chain exists no longer, but I still have that small glass bulb with the mustard seed. It goes with me on any overnight trip, and it is always within easy reach wherever I have lived. There have been times in the middle of the night that I have found myself curled up in a ball on the floor, holding on tightly to my mustard seed, crying out in the darkness for faith and goodness and relief. Then I pin on a swatch of Gubby's shirt.

I also have Gubby's pocket watch and those reading glasses. I don't usually carry them around with me. But I do know exactly where they are: right beside the larger piece of Gubby's shirt, and Rachel Cassell Cooper's Bible (1839–1902), and Rev. Wesley Matthews's Bible, and the Bible that my Grandmother Marvyl Berry Fields gave me back in 1980 when I graduated with my doctorate and that I carried for my second wedding day, and the mustard seed bulb that Pat Fields Matthews gave me forty-one years ago. All of these irreplaceable treasures went with me in the car when we evacuated for Hurricane Irma.

The inspirational theologian and writer Barbara Crafton reminds us that "faith is not an amulet—a magic something you carry around with you to protect you from harm."* Neither the mustard seed that I wear around my neck nor the piece of Gubby's shirt that I pin to my bra are amulets—they do not protect me from harm. They do help to remind me, however, of the place of harm in the overall scheme of my life, to discern what Crafton describes as "the measures of bane and blessing that come our way" and to see them for what they really are . . . and then to draw strength from my ancestors who brought me into this world.

Yes, I keep these treasures, not to protect me from harm, but rather to reassure me of a presence greater than myself in the midst of the worst of it all. Or as Thich Nhat Hanh so eloquently stated in *Living Buddha, Living Christ*, "Whenever I feel sad or a little fragile, I invoke their presence (the ancestors) for support, and they never fail to be there."

. . . .

"Now faith is the substance of things hoped for, the evidence of things not seen."

—Hebrews 11:1 (KJV)

---

*Barbara Crafton, *Geranium Farm Audio eMos*, June 16, 2005.

Full Moon Alert

Let me begin this with a true confession right up front: Halloween is one of my least favorite holidays, and orange is not a color I am particularly attracted to (although having lived in New York City for so many years, I am partial to black). Yet, this holiday is one of the oldest in the world and is still celebrated by adults and children alike. Adults often spend as much on themselves as their children for Halloween, with an amazing $9.1 billion projected to be spent recently in the United States.

Maybe my attitude began with watching *The Curse of Frankenstein* in 1957 which promised to have Frankenstein haunt you forever, and it almost did! (Chalk that one up to my cousin Joni who happened to be visiting us and who not only went to see the movie with me but spent the next week finding endless ways of terrorizing me in his relentless teasing). Skeletons, zombies, ghosts, blood, bones, and violence are not something I enjoy watching on television or reading about in the news. Nope, no *NCIS, Bones, Criminal Minds,* or *CSI: Miami* for me. Anytime my beloved is watching *The First 48 Hours* or *America's Most Wanted,* I walk out of the room.

Perhaps my feelings about Halloween actually go back to my mother. After my younger sister was born, my mom suffered from what we now believe was postpartum depression and became almost debilitated from the illness. We hung in there for three months until finally, once the school year ended, our maternal grandmother came down to Springfield, Ohio, to whisk my older sister and me off to Oberlin, Ohio, for the summer to give our mother a time to heal.

We were promised that we would be back for the first day of school in September. However, mother was not quite back to her old self, and we did not get to go home until her birthday, which was in the first week of October. My sister and I arrived, excited to be rejoined with our family and to return to school; and we eagerly looked forward to the ice cream and cake, the blowing out of candles, and the singing of "Happy Birthday."

Our mother defiantly announced that she would no longer celebrate her birthday on her actual birthday, but rather on Halloween. And so, every Halloween thereafter, we had a devil's food dark chocolate cake with orange icing and a black witch-on-a-broom as decoration. It didn't feel or look like a birthday celebration to me. Where was the yellow cake with white cream frosting decorated with flowers, I wondered. So, I'm not real fond of Halloween. (And, in case the tech savvy among you are concerned, when asked to provide my mother's birthdate in response to a security question, I give a made-up one, which is neither her actual birthdate nor Halloween, perhaps in my own defiance.)

My mother was never quite the same after the birth of my sister. Mom not only held onto her moments of clarity with a vengeance, but also fought like a tigress when she saw that clarity slipping away. At times, she was loving, brilliant, funny, caring, and articulate. At other times, she could become erratic, irrational, and unpredictable. Those times seemed to be heightened by the appearance of the full moon. When Mom was still living, my older sister would call me and say just three words: "full moon alert." It was our code to one another—a warning to be prepared for the unexpected. I then would dutifully put an asterisk in the appropriate square on my wall calendar to prepare me for what would be coming.

Today, my sister and I still alert one another to an upcoming full moon, and we are not alone. Doctors and nurses see full moons as harbingers of chaos, psychotic episodes, and "spooky" births. I don't know if there really is a "The Lunar Effect" or "The Transylvania Effect" around the full moon, but my sister and I certainly have experienced enough of a correlation, both at work and in our personal relationships, to believe that it's true.

Each year on November 1, the Episcopal Church celebrates All Saints' Day, also known as All Hallows Day, and it is a time to honor all saints. On the following day, November 2, the Church celebrates the Commemoration of All Faithful Departed. Those are the two days that I now observe. Halloween, not so much. I stick with the hallowed and the holy.

. . . .

Prayer for the Departed

"Eternal Lord God, you hold all souls in life: Give to your whole Church in paradise and on earth your light and your peace; and grant that we, following the good examples of those who have served you here and are now at rest, may at the last enter with them into your unending joy; through Jesus Christ our Lord, who lives and reigns with you, in the unity of the Holy Spirit, one God, now and forever. Amen."

—Book of Common Prayer

8

One Step Closer
to God

The Potter's House

Music has a magical quality that can mysteriously bring people together, especially in churches. While on a fellowship at Harvard, I often attended Morning Prayer in chapel. The women and men Choral Fellows alternate mornings; Mondays and Fridays they sing together. The service was never long, and the music was often the highlight of our prayer time together.

Among the sixteen Choral Fellows was a young woman with very limited vision. She would follow the sheet music by holding a round magnifier close to the paper with her right hand, her left eye pressed close to the glass. I later learned that she was born with a vision impairment and had perhaps only three or four percent of full vision.

On the days when the women were not singing, she often could be found sitting with the congregants, always on an end seat so that her seeing eye dog could rest close by. The coloring of its coat was the same as her hair, both luxuriously silky and soft.

Sometimes I would find myself sitting near her on the days that she was not singing with the Fellows. Her voice was divine; she sang with the angels. Music to soothe the soul.

One Sunday, I stumbled across a parish in the heart of Boston. I think that if Jesus ever attended church in flesh today, he would surely worship in this parish. What they lacked in finesse, they made up in spirit. I truly felt God's presence: an interracial gospel choir that sometimes sang

Portions of this essay first appeared as "Place for Redemption and Community," in *Seeking God Day By Day* (Cincinnati, OH: Forward Movement, 2013) and "The Potter's House," in *Meeting God Day By Day* (Cincinnati, OH: Forward Movement, 2014). Used with permission.

off-key, but with eyes closed and an open heart; the Lord's Prayer written in both English and Spanish, but prayed aloud in Spanish.

During the Prayers of the People, we prayed for all who had died in the conflicts in Iraq and Afghanistan, for both civilians and for enemy combatants. We prayed for those members of our armed services who had recently lost their lives (and the list was written and read aloud, beginning with John F. Bruner III, 32; Paul D. Carron, 33; Scott J. Fleming, 24 . . . and ending with Erick Yates, 26), "that their deaths may hasten the day when we shall give up war forever."

In the middle of the service, a man with apparent mental illness walked down the center of the aisle and handed the sub-deacon a piece of paper which she took graciously, as they continued with the service, not missing a beat. At Communion, I went up with my purse, mindful of protecting my things; and likewise, the homeless persons in attendance also came up with their roller luggage or carts. At the end the service, there was a toe-tapping, honky-tonk gospel song that we all joined in with praise.

Whether listening to the young lady during Morning Prayer or the gospel choir on that Sunday morning, both were a reassurance that God's hand is in everything and everyone, and that each of us is invited into the potter's house.

. . . .

"Then I went down to the potter's house, and there he was, making something on the wheel. But the vessel that he was making of clay was spoiled in the hand of the potter; so he remade it into another vessel, as it pleased the potter to make."

—Jeremiah 18:3–4 (NASB)

The Kiss

I watched him lovingly and oh-so-gently be accompanied by his daughter toward the chancel, her arm tightly around his waist as they slowly walked, step-by-step. Now eighty-six years of age, Walter was decidedly frail and had begun to sit in one of the back pews rather than his usual place near the front. It was the evening service for Maundy Thursday, the night before Good Friday, and this parish observed the liturgical foot washing, marking Jesus's final act of service in washing the feet of his disciples during the Last Supper.

We had formed two lines, snaking toward the front, the choir's singing of canticles and hymns underscoring the reverent observance. Upon arriving to the front, one person would sit on a chair, while the other (who had just had his or her feet washed) would kneel and begin the ritual: pouring warm water from a pitcher over each foot that was raised above a large bowl, and drying each damp foot with a white cloth. It was an orderly process as volunteers quietly and quickly emptied bowls of water, and provided fresh towels and new pitchers of warm water to each foot washer.

To keep the line moving, we on the left respectfully passed by Walter and his daughter until the two finally reached the front, the last of the congregation to do so. He laboriously sat down first, assisted by his daughter and a priest. Kneeling before her father, she carefully washed and dried each foot. When finished, she and a priest helped Walter back up, and then she sat down in the vacated chair. I wondered what would happen next. Who would or how would the daughter's feet be washed?

Walter stooped over, hands shaking visibly, steadying himself by holding onto a pew. She lifted her left foot high into the air, and a volunteer held the bowl up for an easier reach. He tenderly washed and

148

dried his daughter's left foot, and then we watched as she effortlessly scissored her legs to lower the left foot and raise the right one, which he washed and dried as well. But before she could lower her right foot, Walter leaned down just a little further and he kissed her toes.

He kissed the toes that he had counted at birth. Toes he had kissed when changing diapers. Toes he had kissed when patching up a scraped knee with a Band-Aid. Toes he had kissed after her first pedicure. It was a kiss filled with love, appreciation, adoration, memories, blessings, and thanksgiving. And it was a kiss forever etched in my memory.

For so many years, Walter could be found most Sunday mornings sitting in a folding chair at the entrance to the parish, faithfully welcoming all who entered and offering a bulletin. He was a big fan of Bishop John Shelby Spong, a retired Episcopal bishop of Newark, and I was one of a handful of friends to whom Walter forwarded the bishop's weekly newsletter. I must confess that I did not often actually read the newsletter, but it was always a source of comfort to know that Walter was thinking of me, and that Walter was still with us.

Walter slipped into the waiting arms of God on January 20, 2017. Some of us will remember his sweet smile, or his Sunday morning greeting, or perhaps even the weekly forwarded email. But I . . . I will always remember that Maundy Thursday and the kiss. God rest 'em.

. . . .

"I have set an example that you should do as I have done for you. Very truly I tell you, no servant is greater than his master, nor is a messenger greater than the one who sent him. Now that you know these things, you will be blessed if you do them."

—John 13:16–17 (NIV)

One Step Closer to God

I have already marked the calendar for "pedicure" in anticipation of Maundy Thursday and the foot washing. God always seems to challenge me on Maundy Thursday. On one foot-washing Thursday, I ended up washing the feet of a woman with purple hair, rings in her nose and her tongue, and a tattoo of a snake on her ankle. Yet another year, the man who washed my feet kneeled before me dressed in a pin-stripe suit, starched white shirt, dark red tie, wing-tipped shoes, pocket handkerchief, and horn-rimmed glasses. He ever so gently washed my feet and then embraced me with a "peace be with you." I, in turn, then washed the feet of a young man who was over six feet tall, dressed in blue jeans, and a shoe size an easy twelve. I washed his feet and hairy toes with the same gentleness and care that I had just received.

Back to the pedicure. In anticipation of the foot washing, I always try to remember to get a pedicure a few days before Maundy Thursday. I forgot to make the appointment a couple of years ago. So, there I was, slipping off my shoes and socks, preparing for this very sacred act, and looking down at my royal "va-va voom" blue painted toenails! It had been a long, miserable winter and I—like so many others—longed for spring. On a whim, when I went for my bi-monthly manicure and pedicure, I chose a bright out-of-the-ordinary color to tease me with the promise of warmer weather.

Portions of this essay first appeared as "All in the Name of Love," in *Finding God Day By Day* (Cincinnati, OH: Forward Movement, 2010), and as "One Step Closer to God," in *Meeting God Day By Day* (Cincinnati, OH: Forward Movement, 2014). Used with permission.

Now there I sat in the pew, wondering who was going to be the unlucky person to wash my feet and have to look at my brightly painted blue toenails. In the past, I have had to pray myself through hairy toes, tattoos on ankles, and size twelve feet. But here I was with blue toenails and in the awkward position of wondering what someone else would think of me! After all, I was a member of the vestry, a spiritual director, a retreat leader, a professor . . . with royal blue toenails!

And wouldn't you know it, Sister Ann ended up washing my feet. I watched her big wooden cross swinging across my toes like windshield wipers, as she gently and carefully washed my feet, all with a big smile and a twinkle in her eye.

Yes, Maundy Thursday reminds me that, as we take one step closer to one another, we each take one step closer to God . . . blue toenails and all.

And not to worry, this year my toes will be a respectable pale pink. Remember, I've already made the appointment.

. . . .

"Children of God, people who love one another are coming, all in
    the name of love.
Who am I to say who is a child of God? Who am I to judge?
Dusty feet, dirty feet, calloused feet, tired feet.
Children of God, people who love one another are coming, all in
    the name of love.
Who is this man washing our feet? Who is this Lord, towel in his
    hand? All in the name of love."

—Author Unknown

Holy Greens

A superb athlete all of his life, my beloved had progressed from play-ing football in high school and college to taking up tennis and then golf. Like most things he pursued, he tackled the new sport with concentration, attentiveness, preciseness, and determination—and excelled. He went to golf school, took private lessons, practiced dili-gently almost every day, and joined a golf club. Bringing his handicap down to an impressive low number within a very short period of time, he even won his club championship. On weekends, you would most likely find him on a golf course—either walking the eighteen holes or practicing his chipping and putting. His friends chided him that on Sundays he religiously worshipped at "Holy Greens."

Sunday, May 2, 2002, was fast approaching: the day of Pentecost on the church calendar, the seventh Sunday after Easter, when Holy Eucharist Rite II with Holy Baptism, Confirmation, Reception, and Reaffirmation would be observed at Trinity Wall Street Church located in downtown Manhattan. It was the day that I would officially . . . and finally . . . become an Episcopalian. In a commuter marriage and navi-gating two households in two states separated by nearly 500 miles, I had asked my beloved if he would attend this service in support of my commitment.

Becoming Episcopalian had been a circuitous journey for me, begin-ning when I first arrived in New York City and found myself stopping into the church on my way to work at One Liberty Plaza to light a candle and say a quick prayer. From that very first day, I made a commitment

Portions of this essay first appeared as "Holy Greens," in *Meeting God Day By Day* (Cincinnati, OH: Forward Movement, 2014). Used with permission.

that whenever possible, I would stop in that church to light a candle, to kneel, to pray, to read in the Bible a passage of hope or inspiration. Sometimes, I would just sit in the pew, sighing deeply as tears fell silently down my cheeks.

And then came 9/11, after which I began to attend the noonday service once or twice a week, not quite understanding the ritual but comforted by the familiar singing of "Holy, Holy, Holy," praying the Lord's Prayer, and reciting the Nicene Creed. Raised in the African American Episcopal (A.M.E.) tradition where my father, grandfather, and uncle were all ministers, these Episcopal services were unusually mysterious yet somehow familiar. One Saturday (yes, I often would go into the office on Saturdays for a few hours to catch up), I would quietly stand outside of the small chapel where Morning Prayers were held, lighting a candle and drinking in deeply the soothing prayers. So, I added Saturday mornings to my routine.

Slowly something drew me to the 9:00 a.m. Sunday service, where I found myself sitting in a side pew, entering and leaving without a nod or hello. At 10:00 a.m., off I would quickly depart to hop on the subway to attend the 11:00 a.m. service of my home church, a Presbyterian church, back in Brooklyn. One Sunday, one of the ushers asked me if I had an offering envelope, and when I explained that I was not a member, she just clucked her tongue and said, "Well, you soon will be."

Finally, on a Sunday morning after a 9:00 a.m. service, Father Milton Williams Jr. caught up with me and said very matter-of-factly but oh so pastorally, "You know, God isn't requiring this of you. You need to make a decision, commit, and move on." And so I did.

On Saturday, May 1, 2002, the day before Pentecost, my beloved walked through the front door of our apartment with his overnight bag and a golf bag full of clubs. I inhaled deeply, biting my tongue, and inquired snarkily, "Planning to hit some balls at Chelsea Pier while you're here?"

To which he responded, "Maybe."

(Okay, so I confess that by then I was absolutely livid, with smoke coming out of my ears and lips pursed, askance that he would even *think* about golf on such an important occasion as this for me!)

Sunday morning came and I left the apartment early to attend the prerequisite meeting with the Bishop—a required formality before the confirmation. During the service, as I sat next to my beloved, I could feel my blood pressure rising and my thoughts racing. (How dare he play golf on this day.! There he goes again worshipping at Holy Greens!) I barely could receive the wafer at communion, fearful I might choke on it. As I kneeled before the bishop as he laid his hands on my head in that holy, sacramental moment, I was fearful that lightening might strike me for the resentment clutching my heart.

After the service, we enjoyed a leisurely brunch at a nearby restaurant before heading home. I was unusually quiet. Once home, I immediately took a shower, changed my clothes, and when I came back into the living room, there standing in the middle of the room I saw the set of golf clubs, propped up on its stand, waiting for its next outing.

"Oh?" I asked through gritted teeth, "Are you going to go hit some balls now?"

"No," he responded, with a big smile on his face. "These are for YOU . . . for becoming an Episcopalian."

Golf clubs for becoming an Episcopalian?! Yep. And on that memorable day, my beloved graced me with not only what was important to him but also what he prayed we would share: love of God, a love of each other . . . and a love of golf. And in doing so, I learned a new definition for "Holy Greens."

. . . .

"Golf . . . is the infallible test. The man who can go into a patch of rough alone, with the knowledge that only God is watching him, and play his ball where it lies, is the man who will serve you faithfully and well."

—P.G. Wodehouse

You Just Might Need This

Among my most precious keepsakes are three cards—sealed, addressed, and stamped but never sent: a Mother's Day card; a Father's Day card; and a Valentine's Day card. My mother died on April 25, my father on May 31, and my grandmother on February 14. Thus, cards that were ready to be mailed never made it to their intended recipient. And, after all of these years, I still have those unsent cards, tucked away in a box, joining the stack of every single card that my beloved has ever given or sent to me.

Once, when I was in my 30s and visiting my grandmother, I noticed that she would put aside certain letters or cards during her daily sorting of mail. I asked her why.

"I always keep the most recent letter or card from a special friend or family member," she explained, "in case it becomes the last correspondence that I receive from that person." Wise advice from Nana, and I have done the very same for lo' these many years since.

Saving cards must be a family practice. I remember, soon after my father had died, opening up one of his old briefcases to find every card we daughters and grandchildren had ever given him. Cards both home-made and store-bought filled the briefcase, our names scrawled at the bottom in large print or written with a flourish in script. As I sorted through the collection, I regretted that I had not been a more attentive daughter during the last years of his life, instead choosing to focus on my new marriage and first teaching job.

Yes indeed, correspondence exchanged with loved ones might possibly turn out to be priceless treasures. One of my favorite memories is of first meeting my Great Aunt Reigh at her mother's—my great grandmother (whom we called Muzzy)—funeral. All the family members were in a tizzy, anxiously awaiting Aunt Reigh's arrival, concerned that she would create a "scene" (which I learned later meant that Aunt Reigh did not mince her words, unapologetically slinging her acerbic tongue with sharp precision at her latest target). She finally swooped into the funeral home at the last moment—all decked out in her flashy jewelry, an expensive pastel suit, and a fur jacket draped casually over her shoulders, with a cigarette hanging jauntily between lips—and regally sat down, right in front of me. My mother reached over and touched Aunt Reigh's shoulder while simultaneously nodding toward me (a very frightened thirteen year old who was furiously trying to figure out how to miraculously disappear), whispering, "Aunt Reigh, Aunt Reigh, THIS is the one who looks like YOU."

Aunt Reigh quickly turned around, took one look at me, squinted her eyes, turned back around, reached down into the depths of her purse, and pulled out a five-dollar bill.

"Oh my God," she said, as she thrust the money toward me, "Take this. You're going to need it!" And then unceremoniously turned back around as the brief funeral service began.

Over the years, Aunt Reigh and I became dear friends. Always a planner, by the time she entered her nineties, she had already picked out her burial dress as well as her casket several years prior, and had personally delivered the dress to the funeral home. On an early October morning nineteen years ago, she took her last breath at the age of ninety-four. On the evening of her wake, I quietly stepped up to the open casket and serendipitously tucked a small envelope down along the inside of the lining.

The ever-observant funeral director came over to me to whisper in my ear, "Leaving a little note for Reigh?"

Quietly smiling to myself, I only nodded in response. In the envelope, I had slipped a five-dollar bill with a handwritten note that said, "Here you go, Aunt Reigh. I think you're going to need it."

I can just imagine Peter standing at the Pearly Gates, greeting my auntie with a "Hand it over, Reigh" while they both shared a good laugh.

Send the notes and cards, my friends. And be sure to save the last correspondence you receive from special loved ones. Who knows, you might be expected to produce one of those cards yourself one day!

. . . .

"There are memories that time does not erase . . . Forever does not make loss forgettable, only bearable."
                                        —Cassandra Clare, *City of Heavenly Fire*

Something Greater
Than You and I

When I was ready to apply to college, my parents had only three requirements: 1) it must be a four-year program; 2) it must be affordable to them; and 3) it must be within a fifty-mile radius so that they could drive me to and from college as needed. It narrowed the possibilities, and I settled on a Catholic university about thirty miles from home.

Our family was Methodist; African Methodist Episcopal to be exact. Ours was an equal-opportunity family for worshipping (e.g., Baptist, Pentecostal, Presbyterian, Unity, Unitarian, non-denominational, and Quaker services, and I even attended a Passover seder), although most Sundays I was sitting in the front pew with my mother and siblings while my father, Rev. Wesley Matthews, preached from the pulpit. Attending a Catholic university where the nuns were in charge of the girls' dormitory and where the brothers and the priests taught the classes was all new to me.

Indeed, I never gave much thought to differences in denominations until other students would ask me if I were Catholic. When I told them I was Methodist, they responded matter-of-factly, "Oh, you don't smoke, dance, or drink." (Really? I'd better quick tell my parents, I thought to myself.)

On my first trip home to visit with my family, I asked my father to explain what this all meant . . . these different denominations. I figured he must surely know, being an ordained minister and all.

"Well, the way I think about it," explained my father, "is that for centuries all over the world people have believed in something greater than themselves. To me, that is proof that there is a God."

His simple explanation worked for me, and I have continued to draw upon many faith traditions in my own contemplative practice and teaching; from the works of not only the desert fathers and mothers but also the likes of Thomas Merton, Brother Lawrence, Dorothy Day, John O'Donohue, Henri Nouwen, Hafiz, Parker Palmer, Richard Rohr, Pema Chodron, the Dalai Lama, Thich Nhat Hanh, Elie Wiesel, Rabbi Lawrence Kushner, Howard Thurman, Martin Luther King Jr., and Peter Gomes, to name only a few.

It should come then as no surprise that I was particularly saddened by the three racist attacks that ironically occurred during Ramadan in 2017 (May 26–June 26), a time when Muslims pray, fast, and celebrate the Prophet Muhammad's reception of the divine revelation of the Qur'an. These were three vicious and tragic attacks: a Muslim teen murdered outside a Virginia mosque; a van plowed into worshippers near two London mosques; and two men killed on a Portland train while trying to defend Muslim teens from racist comments.

In the midst of this sadness, I begin to wonder how it is that others do not share my father's simple faith that God exists, even in the midst of this seemingly increasing divide and intolerance of different religions. Are we not a civilized society?

. . . .

"In a civilized society, diversity in religious orientation should be the reason for celebration, not the cause for hatred and differentiation."
—Abhijit Naskar

Finding God at Starbucks

On a spiritual retreat that included thirty-six hours of sacred silence, I began my daily ritual of walking one morning only to be confronted by an unexpected dilemma. My usual walking route took me through a wooded area to a residential community and eventually to Starbucks. Having the time to enjoy a cup of coffee and read *The New York Times* was a great luxury for me—a welcome respite from typically busy days back home. On this particular Sunday morning, I was torn about whether or not I could go to Starbucks and still maintain sacred silence. Slipping folded bills and a note ("grande decaf, leave room for milk") into my back pocket, I started out on my walk. As each footstep drew me closer to Starbucks, questions arose. Can silence be found at Starbucks? Is there sacredness in a cup of java? Is it sacrificial not to have the coffee? Will it be a higher ground or higher grounds?

Somewhere along the way, I began to think that perhaps I was searching for answers about something that did not require this much angst in my soul. God is not in the cup of coffee. God is in ME. If my questioning is centered on the so-called godliness or ungodliness of having a cup of coffee, it would seem that I am missing the more compelling question around "to be or not to be" one with God. "Let the beauty we love be what we do," wrote thirteenth-century Persian teacher and poet Rumi. "There are hundreds of ways to kneel and kiss the ground." Yes, there are hundreds of ways to be with God. God can be experienced

---

Portions of this essay first appeared as "Finding God at Starbucks," in *Sacred Journey: The Journal of Fellowship in Prayer* 58, no. 6 (December 2007/January 2008). Used with permission.

kneeling by one's bedside, kneeling in a pew, or "kneeling" in the bathroom stall at work. It can be experienced kissing a loved one, "kissing" the air, or "kissing" a cup of Starbucks coffee. It is not important where we kneel but that we kneel. It is not important how we kiss but that we kiss. What is most important is that we continually strive to do God's will in all of our ways, and "let the beauty we love be what we do."

For many years, I worked on Wall Street. Finding God at Starbucks is a much easier task than finding God in a stock quote, in a merger or acquisition, or in an Excel spreadsheet. Can spirituality be in the workplace when the job is so financially driven? When I began my studies in spiritual direction, I sensed an open and honest suspicion from my classmates—many wondering how someone from the financial industry could be interested in nurturing a spiritual heart or what kind of calling to the ministry of "holy listening" this might be. Initially, some even questioned whether people in business could be religious and moral. In their minds, contemplation of spirit simply could not occur when one is paid to contemplate profit and loss statements. Skepticism abounded openly and prayerfully—and I humbly embraced it, searching for reaffirmation that I was in the right place at the right time. The call upon my heart to become a spiritual companion came out of a desire to deepen my relationship with God and to companion others in the business world who share a similar desire.

Let me close this where I began—on my way to Starbucks. That Sunday morning, on a hot summer day in early July, I did go into Starbucks and order my cup of coffee, thanking God for the hands that prepared and served it, and blessing the hands that were holding the cup. I have long since returned home from my retreat but I have continued my early morning walk—or now bike rides—and my tradition of having coffee I have brewed at home in my four-cup drip. I have concluded that it is possible to find God at Starbucks, at our jobs, in our work; through our calling because God is with us and within us . . . we take God wherever we go.

. . . .

"No matter what historians claimed, BC really stood for 'Before Coffee.'"

—Chester Sinclair

9

Treasured Memories

Those Were the Days

Labor Day 2016 weekend, I went back to my little village of 3,400 for my—gulp—50th high school reunion. Yellow Springs, Ohio, was and is still a small town known for its hospitality, downtown shops, a vibrant arts community, and "unique" restaurants (think vegan and macrobiotic), with a wide range of political and social views (from John Bachtell, union organizer and chairman of the Communist Party USA since 2014, to the stalwart Republican Richard Michael "Mike" DeWine, former U.S. Senator, former Ohio State Attorney, and now Governor).

There you will find the Little Art Theatre, Glen Helen, Ye Ol' Tavern, the Young's Jersey Dairy, and yes the "yellow spring," which in the 1800s was known for its curative properties. It is the home of comedian and actor Dave Chappelle as well as Antioch College (where Coretta Scott King, Leonard Nimoy, Rod Serling, Virginia Hamilton, Sylvia Nasar, and Congresswoman Eleanor Holmes Norton are just some of the many distinguished alumni).

A week before the reunion, among the incidents dutifully detailed in the weekly newspaper's Village Police Report: a caller required assistance retrieving a cord from under his bed; another caller reported a TV in the middle of the street on Spring Glen Drive; and still another caller found money on the bike path and turned it over to the police. There were goats that made their way back to their home on Corry Street, and the police assisted a homeowner who was locked inside her home due to a faulty deadbolt. There also was a Fairborn male who was cited for possession of marijuana and paraphernalia after being busted with "the devil's lettuce" on Dayton and High streets. Yes, I was home again.

So, imagine my surprise when I heard through the Yellow Springs grapevine that the annual tradition of a family gathering for the New Year's Eve ball drop on Short Street deteriorated into a police altercation when three police cars in full sirens began to disperse the crowd aggressively just after midnight. There was even a reported use of a taser (what? a taser used in Yellow Springs?!). On Monday, January 2, more than one hundred people gathered at the First Baptist Church organized by the 365 Project to express their distress and concerns about police/community relations. By Tuesday, a special Council meeting was held and the police chief had resigned.

It sure is a far cry from the days when James A. "Jimmy" McKee was our police chief. A fixture in the community, he was with the Village Police for thirty-six years (thirty-four as chief) before his retirement in 1993. Among his many accolades, Chief McKee was the first black chief of police of a majority community in the United States, which got him into *Ebony* magazine, a really big deal back then.

One morning in the mid-1960s, Chief McKee came by our house on Pleasant Street to speak with my mother. He needed to take away the plant that was flourishing so well in the clay pot on our front porch. Mom became quite upset. "Why, just this past spring some nice Antioch students were walking by and gave it to me," she proudly reported.

Mom loved that plant and enjoyed boasting about her newly acquired green thumb to anyone who would listen: the plant was growing so quickly, the leaves were so green, and the flowers were blooming like crazy. Chief McKee told Mom that as much as she liked the plant, she could not keep it because it was a cannabis plant. Mom still couldn't understand what the problem was, wondering if it was something like the aloe vera plant that we kept in the house for its many natural health properties. Chief McKee patiently explained to her that her newest plant was considered to be illegal. She was growing pot on our front porch.

"Jimmy," Mom said, "it's a really nice plant that was never going to be used for anything bad."

"I know, Pat; it's a mighty fine plant and you have taken really good care of it," Chief McKee responded as he slowly stepped down off the porch, plant in hand. Carefully placing it on the floor of the back seat of the patrol car, he drove off with a wave and a "You have a good day now."

No tasers, no sirens, no arrests; just a good ol' fashioned conversation and a peaceful confiscation of the contraband. Now those were the days.

. . . .

"Enjoy yourself. These are the 'good old days' that you are going to miss when they're gone."

—Anonymous

Nana, Grandmother, and Big Momma

My visits to my grandmother started when I was in my early twenties. I would make my yearly summer visit to my grandmother and stay for about three days. Nana would pull out her favorite recipes for me to copy. I'd pull out the old scrapbooks to pore over pictures of family members long passed. I'd turn her mattresses, change her light bulbs, and clean out her kitchen cupboards. She'd find some family heirloom to pass along to me—a salt and pepper shaker, a handmade quilt, a tea set. There was more than fifty years age difference between us, but for a few days I felt as though we were sisters, sharing secrets late into the night.

On the last night of my visit I would ask Nana what I should do next. Her advice never ceased to amaze me. I guess with her well-seasoned years, she didn't feel the obligation to mince words. "Lose weight—you're getting too fat." Or "Gain weight—you're getting too skinny." Or "Quit moving around so much—settle down." Or "Hurry up and finish your doctorate and get a job."

Then, Nana began to ask *me* what *I* wanted to do next. What a turn of events! Suddenly, *she* was asking *me*. Still, I was always caught off guard. One would think I would spend the year preparing for the question, but I never did.

First, I said I wanted to do good research and be published in prestigious journals. That's the year Nana told me to go ahead and do the second postdoctoral research fellowship. (I know, I know, no one does two postdocs; except her granddaughter.) The second year I said I wanted to buy all new underwear; I was so very tired of nickel and diming my life away. That was the year she told me to go out and get a real job that paid good money. The third year I told her I wanted to buy a queen-size bed; I wanted the best-dressed bed I could imagine, having pulled out a studio couch for the previous two years. That's the year she told me to go spend money.

Then came the summer I told Nana that what I wanted to do was to get to know myself better. I was on a journey to find myself. I thought an eighty-nine-year-old woman wouldn't understand. Instead, her blue eyes pierced my brown ones as she cocked her hearing-aid side toward me and said with a sigh of relief, "Finally." That was the summer she told me to save my money; I was going to need it soon.

I always wished I were as wise as my grandmother. Yet every year I got older, she got that much older and every year I got a little wiser, she got that much wiser. If only I could see myself as clearly as she did. But then, what are grandmothers for if not to hold a candle at the end of the path to light the way? Nana beckoned me and encouraged me, wrapped my knuckles when I was wrong, and applauded my achievements when I did well. She was always there, waiting with open arms to love her granddaughter. She was my Nana . . . my role model on how to be a grandmother.

I am a grandmother now, but they are only seven and eight. I can only hope and pray that I will remember the lessons of my Nana to pass on . . . to teach them what it means to be a grandmother.

. . . .

"Everybody has a Big Momma; the mother or grandmother who tells it like it is, keeps it real with them, isn't afraid to tell you the truth about yourself."

—Martin Lawrence

One Stitch at a Time

This past Sunday, I rolled over in bed, so tempted to worship at the Church of the Holy Comforter that morning. The hot, humid, and lazy days of summer were finally here, and I had only recently brought out the quilt—handmade by my great grandmother Muzzy—to put on my bed. Light in weight, it's the perfect summer quilt. I wish I could tell you the pattern, but I am afraid I cannot. The pinks and greens on the off-white background carefully and lovingly hand stitched by a woman I only vaguely remember is somehow comforting and reassuring. It is the perfect covering to bury oneself under for an extended sleep.

I have several other quilts that Muzzy made, the one most precious given to me by my grandmother, Nana, forty-eight years ago. Not a particularly pretty quilt, it has black silk as the background with scraps of material from clothing pieced together in some intricate pattern. Sometimes soaking it with tears, sometimes hugging it with unimaginable joy—this particular quilt is so very, very special to me. Indeed, it is so special that I have only loaned it out twice to family members, each time anxiously awaiting its return. Given that the women ancestors in my family were prayer warriors, I know that every stitch in these quilts is filled with their prayers.

I have made a few quilts in my lifetime. My cousin Pat taught me how to make a "cheat" quilt. It is only crib size, and the trick is to find a pattern that has designs around which I can stitch. Thousands of stitches are required. My stitches are not always even, and end knots sometimes show, but each quilt is filled with time, love, and prayers. When I can finally begin to turn the borders and commence the final stitching, I find myself already beginning to think about the next quilt and who might be the recipient.

Indeed, in early March, I finally completed a quilt that I began almost two years ago. That quilt was for my sister, having planned to give it to her for her previous birthday. Life intervened, however, and I was only able to complete it for this year's birthday. Other quilts have been lovingly made for the then infant son of one of my best friends (David is now married with three children of his own), one for my infant niece who is now a new mother herself, one for my first infant granddaughter, and one for my beloved who did not use it ("it's too small, I need a longer and wider one") which I now use as a lap quilt for my morning devotions and evening TV watching.

I've already begun to look at materials for my next quilt. The selection must be made carefully because it is something I will have to live with for many months to come. Pastels catch my eye right now but I won't know until I go into the fabric store and discover what's available and what speaks to me. Or maybe I will undertake a larger sized quilt for my beloved so that he too will have something to throw over him while watching TV.

I have two other keepsakes, handmade, that I treasure; both were needlepointed. A dear high school friend, Marty, needlepointed and framed a small wall hanging that reads, "Learning Never Ends" with "Westina Matthews, Ph.D." and the date of the conferring for my doctorate. I never hung my diploma on any of my office walls, choosing instead to place her gift on the wall. I have a small table lamp for which my great aunt cross-stitched the pattern for the base. (I'm still not quite sure how it was done, although it appears to be a plastic base that allowed the finished product to slip into it.) I remember her spending countless hours working on the piece, and later dusting the lamp in their bedroom in Chicago. She gave it to me as a gift some thirty-plus years ago when I relocated to New York City. It now sits on an end table by my couch in a small TV room at home where I find myself sitting most evenings. Quilt over my lap, lamp on the stand to my left, framed needlepoint hanging on the wall. This has become my prayer room.

One doesn't receive too many handmade gifts anymore, we are all so busy ordering pre-made items online, or purchasing something that says "handmade" by some stranger, often from an even stranger, far away land. So, I will count Muzzy's quilts, Marty's wall hanging, and Betsy's lamp among my priceless treasures, hoping that some family member will treasure them one day as much as I do.

. . . .

"Where your treasure is, there will your heart be also."

—Matthew 6:21 (KJV)

Summertime

I got caught in an unexpected summer shower during my early morning bike ride the other day, the clouds opening up with quite a downpour. Seeking shelter under the moss-covered live oak trees, it was all for naught as my shorts and top became drenched. The temperature was in the mid-70s, the rain was not harsh, and I was able to laugh at my temporary predicament.

It reminded me of my childhood, when, should unexpected summer rain showers hit, our mother would hurry my sister and me into our swimsuits and bathing caps to go play in the rain. We would laugh and shout with glee at the coolness of the rain splashing on our faces and bodies, the fresh grass wet beneath our feet.

We did not have central air or even window air conditioners back then, only one big, round floor fan that had three speeds—low, medium, and high. Midday, in the heat of the summer, my mother would pull all the shades down on every window in our two-story house, and have us stretch out on the floor in the living room, our heads pointed toward the fan, while we took very long naps, the sound of the whirling blades lulling us to sleep.

Summertime in the 1950s was when my father brought out his blue-and-white seersucker suits worn with short-sleeved white shirts. For picnics and at parks, he would wear Bermuda shorts with his long black socks that came over his calves up to his knees. We would giggle to see Daddy's knees, only on view in the summer. Mother wore sleeveless

Portions of this essay first appeared as "Falling Out the Tree," in *Finding God Day By Day* (Cincinnati, OH: Forward Movement, 2010). Used with permission.

blouses and long, flowing cotton skirts, and dressed her daughters in shorts with halter tops or blouses that had elasticized flounce in woven fabric at the top with eyelet embroidery.

No pajamas required at night, we were allowed to sleep only in our panties, with only a sheet to cover us. That is until Nana came to visit and whispered to us that "nice young girls" don't sleep in only their underwear, and she made us cotton summer PJ tops to wear with our panties.

Summer meant enjoying fresh raspberries, blueberries, strawberries, corn, tomatoes, green beans, and lettuce picked from our garden; or roasting hot dogs on a stick over a fire barrel in our back yard; or making s'mores for dessert (I liked my marshmallows burnt to a crisp). It meant that we ate outside most of the time at the picnic table in our back yard. Summer also meant that we could have watermelon for dessert with permission to spit the seeds out on the ground with abandon. (To this day, I will not eat watermelon until *after* the Fourth of July because my father, who grew up in the South, had declared that watermelon was fit to be eaten only after Independence Day when they were sufficiently ripe.) In the dusk of the evening, we would make necklaces and bracelets out of dandelions, and catch fireflies in jars.

We rarely went swimming back then. You see, before we moved to Yellow Springs, Ohio—where everyone was welcomed at the pool at Gaunt Park, named after the former slave Wheeling Gaunt who purchased his own freedom—the only pool that we were allowed to use was the local YMCA in Springfield, Ohio. At this particular Y, there was a certain week each summer that "coloreds" were allowed to come to take lessons from "colored" instructors. Over the summers, I was able to learn how to float, but I never gained enough confidence to swim in that chlorine-filled pool whose shallowest depth still came well over my head. Besides, our mother didn't want us to get our hair wet, and only allowed us to wear our hair natural for that one week each summer (a welcomed relief from the weekly ritual shampooing, air drying, and then using the hot comb with Dixie Peach Pomade to straighten our hair).

Summer was also the time that we piled into Daddy's tan sedan and drove up to Oberlin, Ohio, to visit Mom's family. That visit often included a trip over to Lake Erie—driving up Highway 58 to Lorain County—to find the path our Aunt Faith would show us nestled among the trees and bushes where "colored" could swim. There we could play in the lake with our cousins or run along the beach. Sand between our toes, building sand castles with our buckets, listening to squeals of other colored families splashing in the water, we didn't have a care in the world.

One of my favorite stories about summer passed along to me by my mentor, the Rev. Dr. Paul Smith, is about the theologian Howard Thurman who, as a young boy, was all ready for his summer. School was out, he had a job bagging groceries at the local store, and he was going to play baseball with his friends. On the first day after school was out, he climbed up his grandmother's tree in her back yard to pick some apples, fell out of the tree, and broke his arm.

Arm in a cast, he wondered to his grandmother how there could be a loving God who would allow him to break his arm and destroy all his plans for summer. Why would God punish him like this? To which his grandmother wisely replied, "I think you broke your arm because you fell out the tree."

Yes, summertime is filled with sweet memories of days long past, especially brought to mind while seeking cover under old live oak trees on a morning bike ride. May your summer be filled with loving memories, uneventful mishaps, and everything good.

. . . .

"Everything good, everything magical happens between the months of June and August."

—Jenny Han

Now I Lay Me

As a young child, my parents taught me to kneel by the bed at night and to recite my prayers. My childhood prayer began "Now I lay me down to sleep, I pray the Lord my soul to keep. . . . " I would then end with "God bless Mommy, God bless Daddy" and the list would continue for blessings before the Amen at the end. When I was no longer tucked into bed—and I realized the prayer concluded with "If I should *die* before I wake, I pray the Lord my soul to take"—I stopped kneeling and only quickly prayed the first two lines with a couple of "God blesses" thrown in.

Raised in the A.M.E. church where my father, the Rev. Wesley Matthews, pastored, we would kneel at the altar on the first Sunday of each month to receive communion. Sometimes just before the end of the service, my father would invite members of the congregation to come up and pray in an "altar call," reminding us to bring our burdens to the Lord and to *leave* them there. One of my last images of my father before he died at the age of 68 was of his kneeling by his bedside at night to pray.

On 9/11, after running down thirty-four flights in the World Financial Center and over the Brooklyn Bridge in forty-five minutes (Jackie Joyner Kersee had nothing on me!), I witnessed people stopping to fall on their knees, exhausted and grateful that they had been able to get away from the twin towers. As we approached them, we shouted "GET UP, GET UP," not because we weren't also exhausted and grateful but because there were hundreds of others coming close behind us as we all ran to safety.

On the night before he was crucified, Jesus kneeled with his disciples in the Garden of Gethsemane at the foot of the Mountain of Olives. And on February 1, 1965, in Selma, Alabama, Dr. Martin Luther King Jr.

led a group of civil rights workers and residents in prayer after they were arrested and before being taken to jail for parading without a permit, bending down on his left knee.

Today, as an Episcopalian, I am invited to kneel during the prayers of the people, while saying the general confession and receiving absolution, during the Great Thanksgiving, to receive communion at the altar rail, during the prayer of thanksgiving after communion, and to receive the blessing. It's a lot of kneeling but I receive comfort and reassurance in this ritual. I vividly recall one November answering an altar call at a predominantly black parish in Atlanta, Georgia, and finding myself sobbing uncontrollably while feeling gentle hands resting on my shoulders and head as fervent prayers were whispered over me.

The Denver Broncos quarterback Tim Tebow, a devout Christian, is known for falling to one knee, arm resting on the other knee, with head bowed and praying before a game starts; it even has a name—"teebowing." Yet, after Colin Kaepernick, the former quarterback for the San Francisco 49ers, whose body displays multiple religious tattoos including a cross and one with praying hands, began to take a knee during the singing of the national anthem in protest of social injustice, he now no longer belongs to a team. Tebow is revered while Kaepernick is reviled.

I have often heard that courage is just fear saying its prayers. Falling down on your knees, kneeling, taking a knee, Jesus praying with the disciples, Dr. King praying with civil rights workers, and world events today—it's all enough to make me start getting back down on my knees at night to pray, reciting that *entire* childhood prayer I learned so many years ago.

> Now I lay me down to sleep,
> I pray the Lord my soul to keep,
> If I should die before I wake.
> I pray the Lord my soul to take.

· · · · · · · · · · · · ·

"There comes a time when one must take a position that is neither safe, nor politic, nor popular, but he must take it because conscience tells him it is right."

—Martin Luther King Jr.

Sunday Ironing

I usually do the laundry on Saturdays; and then on Sundays after church, I iron. I know, I know, hardly anyone irons anymore. But I do.

Perhaps I bring out the ironing board, iron, spray bottle, and spray starch because it reminds me of my childhood when my mother would iron. We had one of those old-fashioned top-loader electric washing machines with a wringer. During nice weather, the washer could be found on our back porch; and during the winter, the washer was placed in our oversized bathroom. Clothes needed to be hung outside to dry with wooden clothespins on the clothes lines stretched from our porch to the garage, or brought inside during inclement weather.

On the night before ironing day, Mom would pour a small pan of cold water, dissolving Argo starch in the water, and then begin to sprinkle, roll, and place the clothes in the refrigerator to chill. (I still remember as a child, sneaking under the kitchen sink to find that starch to sprinkle on a sliced orange. I'm sure that wasn't good for me but I seemed to crave the taste.)

The next morning, Mom would set up the ironing board and iron in the dining room; and she would spend most of the day ironing away. She took pride in ironing Daddy's crisp, white shirts and her daughters' dresses with the big sashes. When I became old enough, she taught me how to iron my father's white handkerchiefs; and later she showed me how to iron shirts and blouses (start with the collar band, move to the sleeves carefully ironing the cuffs, next the yoke, and lastly the front panels, giving special attention to the button holes).

We did not have a lot of money but Mom was industrious. She sure could make a dollar stretch for sure—from selling bouquets of freshly cut flowers from our yard on Memorial Day to taking in ironing for white ladies who lived in the "rich" neighborhood.

By then I was in the second grade, attending Highland Elementary School (a recently desegregated school in Springfield, Ohio) as one of a handful of "coloreds" and had developed an interest in drawing. I was better at drawing flowers and trees than people. One of my classmates, Anne, could draw the best profiles of Veronica Lodge from the Archie comic book series. Inspired, I tried to do the same with little success. I asked Anne if she would teach me and she agreed on one condition: every school day, upon her arrival to school, I was to take her coat and hang it on her designated hook in the cloak room, and then fetch her coat for recess and at the end of school day. That was it?!! What a bargain, I thought.

This went on for several weeks, and at the end of each week Anne would spend about ten minutes teaching me how to draw Veronica. She also gave me a slip of paper about the size of a check with a "made payable to" and her signature on the front and a sketch of Veronica (full figured) on the back. My drawings began to improve.

Then one day, my mother was cleaning out my very cluttered desk at home and discovered my Veronica stash. She gently inquired about them, and I proudly explained about my drawing lessons. Mother waited until Daddy got home, they talked, and the next day Daddy drove Mom to school to pick me up.

Mom was waiting at the classroom door when school was dismissed, quickly hugged me and then went in to speak with my teacher. I wasn't sure what was going on, but I noticed the teacher kept apologizing profusely and her face was quite flushed. We then got in the car and drove over to the rich white neighborhood.

Daddy stayed in the car while Mommy asked me to come with her. I wondered if we were picking up more ironing for mother to do. But no, we were at Anne's house. Anne's mother answered the door (I recognized her from when she brought cookies for snack time at school) and my mother proceeded to "bless her out." I heard words like "maid" and "servant" and "recess." Anne was called to the door and made to apologize to me, and then had to promise to end our arrangement immediately.

Mom dragged me back to the car, slammed the door, and used some pretty choice curse words to tell my Daddy what transpired. I hunkered down in the back seat, grateful to have those few lessons on how to draw

Veronica. Not surprisingly, Anne never spoke to me, let alone looked at me, again.

It was several years before I learned what a maid was (perhaps by seeing Annie Johnson—played by Juanita Moore—in the 1959 release of the movie *Imitation of Life*?) or to truly comprehend what Anne had been asking me to do. Mom continued to take in ironing and I began to try to teach myself how to draw. To this day, I still don't draw people too well, sticking to mostly flowers and trees; but I do love to iron on Sundays. No Argo starch, but I still iron my blouses the same as I was taught those many years ago: start with the collar band, move to the sleeves carefully ironing the cuffs, next the yoke, and lastly the front panels, giving special attention to the button holes.

I find it somehow soothing as I wait sometimes not so patiently for my great aunt to make her transition. As my friend Patti reminded me at coffee hour, "We're all okay with dying; it's the getting there that's so difficult." Ironing helps me get there.

. . . .

"I find it soothing to take something wrinkled and make it smooth. It feels anticipatory. It's what I do before a celebration. And nobody bothers me when I'm ironing."

—Alexandra Stoddard

The Way We Were

This year, I thought I might make my homemade rolls for Thanksgiving dinner. I hadn't baked anything since Hurricane Matthew, so I was long overdue to bring out some baking pans. I remember a Christmas years ago when I went home to Yellow Springs, Ohio, to visit with my family. I had not been home since my then recent divorce, new Ph.D. status, and move from Chicago to New York City. There had been many changes, and I was anxious to see how the "new me" was accepted.

My mother greeted me with open arms and immediately took me into the kitchen to show me the five-pound bag of flour and packages of yeast that she had purchased. During those first few days at home, my mom kept referring to the flour and the yeast that was waiting for me in the kitchen.

Finally, I couldn't stand the suspense any longer. I asked my younger sister, "What's the scoop on this flour and yeast? Mom keeps referring to the flour and the yeast that she bought for me. For the life of me, I can't image what I'm supposed to do with the stuff!"

And then my sister reminded me, "You used to make the most wonderful rolls when you lived here before. Mom keeps talking about those great rolls, and she was hoping that you make some for us while you're home."

"Rolls?" I responded incredulously. "I used to make rolls? When was this? I don't remember making any rolls!"

I was beginning to panic. Had senility begun to creep in already?

"Oh yes," my sister responded. "They were so delicious. You always made them for holidays and for special occasions."

Somewhere in my memory bank, I began to dust off images of kneading dough and pulling pans of freshly baked rolls out of a hot oven.

Oh, my goodness, I really did do that once. For the life of me, I couldn't remember the recipe, let alone how to push that dough into roll shapes.

The visit was beginning to wear me down. Every time I looked up, my mother would talk about the flour and the yeast that were waiting for me in the kitchen; friends would talk about the weekly trips we used to make to the nearby mall—or try to reminisce about the good times we shared as couples with my "ex."

One morning, I woke up and went down for breakfast. Before us, Mother had placed a feast: pork chops, hash browns, scrambled eggs, grits, gravy, and biscuits. It was a far cry from my usual fare of fruit, yogurt, and coffee. Somehow I finished the meal, forcing the food over my tongue and down my throat, certain my arteries were clogging up with every bite. I put down my fork and cleared my throat.

"Let's talk about what I *don't* do anymore. I don't eat big breakfasts. I don't go to malls. And I don't make rolls anymore!"

My jaw was set in determination, as I left the table and prepared to go into the village (all of two blocks on Xenia Avenue) to run some errands. I began to hum quietly to myself, glad I had cleared the air. Now, maybe they would leave me alone.

Browsing in the variety store, I bumped into a fellow elementary school teacher from my teaching days. We exchanged warm greetings and then she began to talk about faculty meetings, school plays, and parent conferences that we had shared in the past. My eyes began to glaze over as I tuned out my friend. When her mouth finally stopped moving, I smiled and just said, "You know, I don't make rolls anymore."

She looked at me totally perplexed, as I quietly turned on my heel and continued humming softly to myself the same song I had begun earlier that day: Barbra Streisand's "The Way We Were."

This year, thirty-some years later, I dusted off that piece of notebook paper, yellowed and aged around the margins, stained with flour, mashed potatoes, and butter. As I assembled the necessary ingredients, I began reading the first words of the recipe, "First you need a bowl . . ." and under my breath began to hum the very same tune I hummed softly to myself those many years ago in the variety store in Yellow Springs, Ohio.

• • • • • • • • • • • •

"There comes a time in your life when you have to choose to turn the page, write another book or simply close it."

—Shannon L. Alder

Here's Grandma

Completely disoriented in a twin-sized bed, I felt a nose pressed to mine, with a sweet breath blowing on my lips. I opened my eyes to find two small eyes peering at me.

"Are you awake yet, Grandma?" she asked. "Is it time to get up yet?"

Squinting over to the clock on the bedside table, I saw it was only 5:45 a.m. Much too early for me or this little munchkin to be up. I was visiting just before Christmas, arriving for presents under the tree.

"Not quite, sweetheart. Give Grandma another forty-five minutes, okay?"

But as I started to roll over to catch a few more winks, I thought back to a day only seven years ago.

"Where's Grandma?" I heard my daughter ask my nine-month-old granddaughter. Big, brown saucer eyes turned toward me and smiled. My heart broke open in joy and wonder.

As I reached for her, I remembered a conversation that I had with my own mother so many years ago. In one of our late-night telephone conversations, I quietly confessed to her that when I died and got to heaven, the first question that I intended to ask God was why I didn't have any children. How could he have made a woman whose arms ached to hold a child of her own, and yet decide that she was to not have one?

So there, in a whispered confession to my mother, I shared my—until then—unasked question. "Why me, Lord? Why did I never have a child?"

Portions of this essay first appeared as "Here's Grandma," in *Wisdom Found: Stories of Women Transfigured By Faith* (Cincinnati, OH: Forward Movement, 2011). Used with permission.

A prayer partner once reminded me that God's will is what you would choose if you knew all the facts. Because I rarely know all of the facts, I still find myself at times being willful . . . wanting my way, on my timetable. My faith still wavers, and in those times, it becomes difficult to understand—let alone accept—God's will for me.

Yet, fifteen years later, my nine-month-old granddaughter was reaching out her chubby arms to give me a slobbery baby kiss. Handing her over to me was my "adopted" daughter-by-another-mother who entered my life when she was a seventeen-year-old college intern at my job. One evening over dinner, we adopted each other, becoming the family each of us yearned to have but seemed to have been denied.

"Wait, sweetie," I called out to my granddaughter as she resolutely had turned to go back out of the bedroom. "Grandma's up. Let's go downstairs so we won't disturb the others. This will be our time."

Yes, God's will is what you would choose if you knew all the facts.

. . . .

"My grandmother started walking five miles a day when she was sixty. She's ninety-seven now, and we don't know where the heck she is."

—Ellen DeGeneres

Airports, Santa, and Christmas

Sitting in the lounge at LaGuardia one December, I saw fathers or mothers seated beside a daughter or a son, waiting for their planes to be ready to board. The children appeared to be under the age of ten, all seemingly content, undisturbed by the travel arrangements. Busy with iPhones, iPads, or Kindles, the children seemed nonchalant about the wait, obviously seasoned travelers. It's almost Christmas and I begin to wonder if the parent was taking his or her child to or from the other parent, sorely tempted to make up stories about their lives.

Growing up, I can only remember one time that my father traveled without us for an overnight trip. I know he took a train because when he returned, he came back bearing gifts—a toy engine for my sister and a toy caboose for me—and only twice did my parents leave us with a babysitter for the evening. Otherwise, we were a four- and then a five-some (when my younger sister joined us some seven years later), joined at the hip, always together.

I don't know what it is for a child to celebrate Christmas with only one parent. I know what it is to sit around the tinseled Christmas tree, lights out and the big colorful bulbs shining, as we sang all of our favorite Christmas carols and listened to our parents singing "Baby, It's Cold Outside." I know what it is to attend the Christmas Eve service with Sunday school teachers giving us a small red-and-green box, filled with hard candy, complete with a string handle for hanging on the tree. I didn't especially like the hard candy but it was the only time besides Halloween that we were permitted to have that much candy at one time. I know what it is to leave carrots and water for reindeer, and sugar cookies and small glass bottles of Coke for Santa. I know what it is to wake on Christmas morning to see what Santa had left under the tree while our parents watched us unwrap packages with glee.

Then, few families flew on planes; there weren't the plethora of technology devices; and everyone believed in Santa, or at least pretended to believe. Whatever the changes, the magic of Christmas and the traditional carols can still be heard and sung. It's Christmas and the sound of "Joy to the World" can be heard around the world.

· · · · · · · · · · · ·

"Our hearts grow tender with childhood memories and love of kindred, and we are better throughout the year for having, in spirit, become a child again at Christmastime."

—Laura Ingalls Wilder

10

Remember to Breathe

Spaces between the Lines

Two big, dark-chocolate-brown six-year-old soulful eyes looked up at me, hoping that I might like her specially selected Christmas gift for Grandma: an adult coloring book entitled *Whatever Is Lovely: A Coloring Book for Reflection and Worship*. Accompanying the gift was a box of watercolor pencils in twelve assorted colors. Made of water-soluble lead, they could be used dry or be brushed with water to create different shades. I promised my granddaughter that I would use the coloring book and send her photos as proof.

I had heard and read about this new adult coloring book phase; a couple of friends had even sheepishly confessed they had begun coloring, but as yet it held no attraction for me. According to an interview in *The New York Post*, more than two thousand different adult coloring books have hit the stands since 2013 and the genre's two biggest bestsellers, *Secret Garden* and *Enchanted Forest*, had sold a combined 13.5 million copies in fifty countries! Why in 2015 alone, an estimated twelve million adult coloring books were sold in the United States; and while adult coloring books may not be keeping pace with 2015, the books remained popular enough to increase print unit sales of adult nonfiction by twelve percent in the first half of 2016.

And so, I began to color. I had read that coloring offered adults at least seven benefits, but the two that appealed to and motivated me the most—besides, of course, pleasing my granddaughter—was stress relief and mindfulness. Filled with questions, I found my first endeavor into coloring to be neither calming nor soothing. Which colors to choose? How do I stay within the lines? What happens when I apply water to the tip of the pencil? Am I able to do any shading? And just how long is it really going to take for me to finish each drawing?

My particular coloring book promised to provide a way to "quiet the noise, express my creativity, and spend some sweet time with God." Not hardly. Instead, I became caught up in considering complex color schemes that required focus, problem solving, organizational skills, and concentration—which, by the way, turned out to be one of the promised seven benefits of coloring, (i.e., an intellectual benefit). Not interested, no thank you. I don't want to think. I want to *not* think. I want to empty. I want to make room for new meanings and new thoughts.

By the third page, I felt driven to create spaciousness and airiness in the drawings. Drowning in colors and patterns, I desperately needed to feel less obligated to fill in every single, intricate image in those teeny, tiny, small spaces. What had happened to my spirit of spontaneity and freedom? White may not be considered a color in physics, but it is a distinct color in the visual arts. As we all well know, I am not a physicist, but apparently my granddaughter thinks that I have the potential to become an artist. So doggone it, the artist in me was going to start leaving some of those spaces white.

I remember once, after an Alvin Ailey performance, asking Judith Jamison to explain a particular work that ended without any music, the dancers continuing to move in synchronized dance movements with split-second timing on the otherwise silent stage. I was mesmerized by the dancers' feet hitting the floor with precision; watching their heads, arms, hands, and shoulders move to some hidden beat, their torsos leaping high into the air; leaving both the audience and the dancers breathless when they finally bowed to thunderous applause and shouts of "Bravo!"

Judith just smiled at me and replied, "Ah, but there *was* music."

I am now leaving white spaces in the drawings, intentionally untouched and left blank within the lines, yet filled with possibilities and mystery. I am on my sixth page. Om-m-m-m.

. . . .

"But let there be spaces in your togetherness,
And let the winds of the heavens dance between you."
                                        —Kahlil Gibran

This Is My Body

My beloved has just challenged me to lose three pounds a week for the next seven weeks. What planet does he live on? Maybe when I was in my forties or fifties, I could lose at that rate. But today? Cough, snort, gasp for air. Still, I have taken up the challenge with the same enthusiasm I had in my younger days. I've signed up for water aerobics, Pilates, and yoga at the neighborhood fitness center. My bike comes out daily for hour-long rides, and I have reintroduced myself to the weight machines.

But please understand, vigorous exercise has never been my thing, and Jane Fonda and I have never been tight buddies. Years ago I did buy her videotape and book, and tried to exercise religiously for a week. But there was something ludicrous about Fonda asking at the end of each workout, "Now then, don't you feel better?" that managed to drive me absolutely bonkers. Sweat pouring off my body, every muscle aching, gasping for breath—no, I did not feel better. I feel better when I'm curled up on my couch, watching television and sipping a glass of wine. Now, *that* makes me feel better.

And have you seen Jane Fonda lately? Almost eighty years old and looking absolutely amazing. When she was seventy-seven, she observed, "I have a fake hip, knee, thumb; more metal in me than a bionic woman, but I can still do Pilates." Well, I am nowhere near seventy-seven, and I still have my hip, knee, and thumb and no metal; yet, my execution of some Pilates movements could convince me that some body part has been replaced and I was not notified! If it's any consolation—oh, how I enjoyed Lily Tomlin throwing some shade on her costar on the *Today* show when she dryly observed that she'd known Fonda more than fifty years, at least since before Fonda's first face lift!

Still, when I squint my eyes and dare to look at myself in the mirror au naturel, I wonder whose body is this? Cottage cheese thighs, Julia Child arms ("and n-o-w, you s-t-i-r-r), John Wayne hips, hair turning gray on places other than my head (only my hairdresser knows for sure what color my eyebrows really are); and is there some kind of balloon in my stomach that continues to inflate?

Of course, exercise alone won't do it, so I must also watch what I eat as well. That's why I love Lent as a weight-loss tool. Trying to lose weight on my own rarely works; but for God I can do anything. And for my beloved who threw down the gauntlet in a weight-loss challenge, I am willing to give it the old college try.

"Just say no," Nancy Reagan encouraged us to do during the 1980s War on Drugs. While not especially effective then, perhaps "no, thank you" to the tempting desserts proffered at tonight's dinner party just might work for me.

Shantell Hinton, assistant chaplain at Vanderbilt University, wrote that when Jesus sat with his disciples and offered the broken bread, saying, "this is my body," she imagines "this was an equally ironic and ignominious moment of his time on earth. That he must not only give up his body as an instrument of atonement for the guilt of humanity, but also teach those who would be complicit in his demise how to celebrate their redemption at his expense." Rev. Hinton goes on to reflect on her own duality or double-consciousness as she suffers bias, oppression, and prejudice—and how "this is my body" became her own form of a centering prayer.

"This is my body" has become my own centering prayer as I meet the weight-loss challenge. This is the body given to me at birth. I am the shortest and smallest of the members of my family. My skin is of darker complexion and my hair is wavier than those of my sisters. I stare at old photos of my ancestors and relatives, and try to find some resemblance (am I the only child who thought her parents took home the wrong baby from the hospital?). Yet . . . still . . . I have been taught that this is my body that was broken for you (1 Corinthians 11:24 [KJV]). Yes, this is my body. I embrace it lovingly, wholly, and happily.

By the way, my manicurist was alarmed last week at what she thought was a lump on my left wrist. Oh, no it wasn't a lump . . . it was a muscle. Three weeks of exercise and all I have to show for it is a small muscle on my left wrist. Go figure. And now I'm off to my yoga class followed by an aqua lite class this morning. Whether in a leotard, in a swimsuit, patting my thighs, hugging my waist, moving into a downward dog, executing a mermaid in the pool . . . yes, my friends, this is *my* body.

Allow me to end this reflection with a prayer I now recite each night:

Please, please God, do not let him have a perfect body.
Let me find a roll around the waist or a sag in the rear.
A few wrinkles around the eyes or gray in the hair.
An arthritic hip or a bad knee.
A few scars here and there, or a dry patch or two.
Let him be less than perfect, God, let him be like me.
Let him be human, God, just like me.
Amen.

. . . .

"Your mind can deceive you and put all kinds of barriers between you and your nature; but your body does not lie. Your body tells you, if you attend to it, how your life is and if you are living from your soul or from the labyrinths of your negativity . . . The human body is the most complex, refined, and harmonious totality."

—John O'Donohue

Stop, Look Both Ways, Then Go

The best birthday gift that my beloved has ever bestowed upon me is my bicycle—a three-speed, brakes in the feet and hands, fat tires, silver Townie. I love this bike, and ride it around the island almost daily on the seemingly endless bicycle/cart paths, weather permitting. Helmet safely secured, water bottle and a piece of fresh fruit in the front basket, sunglasses perched on nose, handlebar-mounted rearview mirror in place . . . and off I go for at least an hour, if not more. I enjoy the freedom of riding and the challenge of keeping my balance, the lush greenery, kaleidoscope of flowering plants, and scenic river views. (I remember when, as a child, I could ride with no hands on the bars, arms swinging freely beside me; but now find it best to have at least my left hand on the handle to assure I stay upright.)

As a child, my parents taught me to "stop, look both ways, then go" when I came to an intersection. We only had three stoplights in the village of Yellow Springs, Ohio (I believe there are four traffic lights now), and it was long before there were blinking lights that say "walk" or a figure of a person walking, so the "stop, look both ways, then go" worked pretty well. There are no stoplights that intersect with my bike paths, and using the tried but true "stop, look both ways, then go" continues to serve me well.

The only hazardous obstacle on my bicycle rides are the men who drive their golf carts as though they were at the Indianapolis Motor Speedway. Driving fast and furiously with little regard for me or my

Portions of this essay first appeared as "Stepping Out in Faith," in *Seeking God Day By Day* (Cincinnati, OH: Forward Movement, 2013). Used with permission.

bicycle, I am often forced off the path (where in theory bicyclists have the right of way), as they careen past me without a fare-thee-well or a glance back. The other day, I saw a man with an artificial right leg, crossing the intersection to our village stores—where thank goodness there is the sole stoplight—against the light, steering with his left hand while his right hand held tight to the dog that sat precariously on the seat beside him. I just stopped and yielded the right of way. It seemed much safer.

I remember once watching with horror as a young woman bicyclist flipped entirely over and landed on her back in the middle of a Boston street. Thank goodness, she was wearing a helmet. Without hesitation, I ran out to stop traffic, calling out to her to see if she was all right. Dazed, she remained on her back for a few anxious moments while she caught her breath. Two other cyclists stopped and came over to move her bike out of the street, checking to see if she needed assistance as the line of stopped cars began to form behind her.

Suddenly, an automobile began to speed past the other cars, barreling toward us. I yelled out, "Watch it!" The driver nastily shouted out his rolled-down window, "I see it, but I've got to go," whisking by as he accelerated. Thankfully the young lady seemed more shook up than hurt, and finally got up to begin walking her bike home.

Even today, when I am back in New York City visiting, I watch with new appreciation at how people simply ignore stoplights and focus primarily on the traffic flow. While some of the lights now give a seven-second head start for pedestrians at 2,381 intersections in the city, one still must be particularly brave to cross the streets in the Big Apple. If no cars are seen coming, or if pedestrians think they can cross the street before the car is fast upon them, they step out with confidence—daring the car to hit them. It doesn't help that many drivers test their ability to "make" a light, even if it means the car will be stuck in the middle of the intersection, blocking all foot and car traffic.

With envy, I watch younger people step out fearlessly—seemingly unconcerned—trusting that the cars will stop and give them the right of way. In some ways, I envy the self-absorption, sense of entitlement, and swagger of the youth. Perhaps because of age and experience, I have learned that people do not always follow the rules and often try to find a way around them. So now when I approach an intersection, on foot or on bicycle—even if I have the right of way—I first seek eye contact with the driver. *Do you see me? Will you stop? May I cross?* I wait for a nodding acknowledgment, raise my hand in a silent "thank you," and only then do I dare to step out. Or sometimes I just wait until some younger person begins to enter the crosswalk—seemingly oblivious—and follow close behind.

If only I still had the fearlessness of youth. What would my life be like today? Not sure, but on this morning, I will mount my bicycle, take a spin around the island, and simply enjoy the ride. It's my version of cautious fearlessness. Stop, look both ways, then go!

· · · · · · · · · · · ·

"The spirits are low, when the day appears dark, when work becomes monotonous, when hope hardly seems worth having, just mount a bicycle and go out for a spin down the road, without thought on anything but the ride you are taking."

—Sir Arthur Conan Doyle, Sherlock Holmes author

Be Flexible, Celebrate the Journey, Remember to Breathe

After twelve weeks of water aerobics six times per week, yoga three times a week, and Pilates once a week, I can finally lift and rest the ball of my foot on the inside bar of the pool for a good hamstring stretch. Don't laugh. This is quite an accomplishment because when I started this exercise routine, I could only get the foot halfway up the side of the pool. Now, when the yoga instructor asks us to assume the happy baby pose, lying on my back, I can grip the insides of my feet, gently spread my knees open, and stretch my legs out. Oh, and my fingers can curl under my toes in a downward bend. Hip, hip, hooray! I am finally becoming more flexible.

Being flexible at my age is important . . . not only for balance, bone strength, posture, and let's not forget (pun intended) for agility of mind. I say this because I am not being very flexible about a lot that is going on in the world right now. I find myself grimacing, shifting uncomfortably, taking deep breaths . . . anything to prevent me from saying out loud what I am *really* thinking.

Read *The New York Times* . . . up goes my right foot on the inside bar of the pool as I take deep breaths.

Watch the six o'clock news . . . and I move into the lotus seated position with both thighs rotating externally, as my knees begin to flex, allowing the left thigh to be more flexible than the right thigh and pleased that each day knees move a little closer to the ground, half inch by half inch.

Quick glance at the headlines on Apple News on my cellphone . . . lie face up, bring my hands behind my right leg and begin to pull my leg to my face, scissor the legs and then pull the left leg up to my face, and try to remember to breathe. Inhale. Exhale.

Overhear the conversations while standing in line in the grocery store
. . . and I bend over with my knees slightly flexed as my fingers touch my
toes, curling the toes upward as the tips of my fingers slip under.

I have known a lot of dogs in my lifetime, and they weren't canine
. . . they were of the human species. A girlfriend once confessed that she
sent a case of dog food to the workplace of an ex who did her wrong.
Wish I had thought of that. I had a few cases to send. I wonder what
would happen if we all began shipping cases of dog food anonymously
to the two-legged ones in our society today? See, there I go again: jaws
clenching, lips pursed, forehead frowning, and body tightening up. Have
to remember to stay flexible, stay present in the journey, and to *breathe*.

I worry about a society where it seems to be no longer safe to share
your opinions. How did we become so divided with a "them vs. us" men-
tality? How is that we can no longer distinguish between truth-telling
and alternative facts? And what ever happened to due process, or that
you are innocent until proven guilty?

Rachel Naomi Remen wrote that "when you listen generously to
people they can hear the truth in themselves, often for the first time."
When did we become so miserly in our ability to listen to one another?
Where and when will we be able to have difficult conversations again?
Or did we ever?

These are the things that I think about on my bike ride to and
from the fitness center or on long walks around the island, trying not
to let the newspaper headlines, or political pundits, or overheard conversations disturb my equanimity. Instead, I focus on remaining—and
becoming—more flexible, celebrating the small victories of releasing
unnecessary tensions in my body, and hopefully keeping an open mind
and a compassionate heart while I strive to celebrate each moment of
the journey. All prayers invited and needed. Lord knows, I need them.
(Can't you just hear Dionne Warwick singing softly in the background
right about now: "What the world needs now, is love, sweet love. . . .")

. . . .

"The stuff of life may not be ours to understand. It's enough to offer
love, to receive the best and worst, to embrace and say farewell."
—Danna Faulds

Family Reunion

About forty years ago, I went to the Woodson's family reunion one summer. Actually, my linkage to the Woodson clan is through a great-great-great-great, but because my grandmother held such a keen interest in the reunion, about ten of us decided to attend that year with her. There were over two hundred people there from across the country—all shapes, sizes, ages, and colors.

What I enjoyed most about the reunion was that all of the older living members of my family had come together. Grandmother was then 89; there was Great Aunt Reigh who was 77, a great uncle who was 73, and another great aunt who was 70. I could look at them and understand better who I am.

All of the women have what I call "raccoon eyes," little dark circles under the eyes. Oh, how I've tried various lighteners to hide those dark circles—only to finally accept that I will always have them. All of the women have long hair—braids or buns wrapped around their head. Yet, why did I get so annoyed that I have to get my hair cut every six weeks to keep a short haircut? And how could I have forgotten that less than five years prior, I was sitting on my hair? All of our family have high cheekbones. Among those two hundred cousins, our twig on the tree was the only one with those distinctive high cheekbones.

Not only did I learn about who I am, I learned a lot about whom I've come from. The last night together, our family gathered in one of the hotel rooms. My cousin Pat and I got out our pens and paper and

Portions of this essay first appeared as "Family Reunion," in *Finding God Day By Day* (Cincinnati, OH: Forward Movement, 2010). Used with permission.

made the oldest members of our family go through the family line. As Pat wrote down the names and dates, I wrote down the anecdotes.

I wondered what two or three sentences would be attached to those relatives sitting in that hotel room on that night. For every family member, there were two or three sentences always repeated. Grandma Hale ate her dinner with a long fingernail file and in black gloves. Grandpa Cooper had long flowing hair down to his shoulders and wore a tall hat.

If each of us had our say, what would we choose to have remembered about us? Grandma Hale did not begin eating dinner with a fingernail file until she was in her 90s and senile. Yet, that's what has been passed along for more than seventy-five years.

Will we be remembered for our best and noblest deeds or for our greatest failures? Will we only be remembered for how we lived out the end of our lives, rather than the beginning or the middle? Who writes our history? And who chooses to remember it?

I told Pat that I thought everyone would remember that she lived in a twenty-one-room house with a swimming pool. "Don't you think anyone will remember that I was a trustee for ten years for the major state university, and chairman of the board?" she asked sadly.

"Well, we'll make sure they do," I responded, and I wrote down next to her name about the trusteeship. I then began to think about what I wanted written by my name. I have yet to write anything. I mean, I only have two sentences. It would seem that my life is not over yet. I am only in Act II, Scene II.

. . . .

"Life's like a play; it's not the length but the excellence of acting that matters."

—Lucius Annaeus Seneca

One Breath at a Time, One Moment at a Time

The other week, I was in the grocery store looking at the dates on the milk bottles. November 16. They all said November 16. Disgusted, I put the milk carton in my basket. Why do I have to buy milk with the expiration date the same as today?

After I got home, as I began to put my groceries away, I glanced over at the calendar and saw that today's date was actually November 12. The twelfth? Oh my gosh, I thought it was the sixteenth!

I sat down on my couch in amazement. I could chalk this up to being retired and not as calendar- or appointment-bound as I had been when I was working full time. If I were honest with myself, I would confess that there I go again, thinking that I had run out of time—which seems to be a more frequent thought as I grow older. Like the white rabbit in *Alice's Adventures in Wonderland*—who cried out, "Oh dear! Oh dear! I shall be too late!"—I seem to spend more time scurrying along, thinking that I've run out of time, and following that gosh darn rabbit down its hole.

I'm much better about my yesterdays. I've pretty much shut the door on my past and filed it under History. But my tomorrows? All too often I'm thinking about the future, the what ifs and the why nots; and therefore, I tend to miss so many wonderful moments in my today. Sometimes, I find myself tapping my foot or clapping my hands or snapping my fingers to consciously bring me back into the present moment.

One friend suggested that I "be where my feet are," and that I had very smart feet, so I should just follow my feet. Another friend gently reminded me that "you can't take your two o'clock breath at a quarter to two." What a nice turn of the phrase. I suppose the reverse is true, too: you can't take your quarter of two breath at two o'clock either.

But why, oh why, does right now sometimes feel like forever always? Perhaps that very thought is why I rush along, convinced that I don't know how much time I have left. Yes, it only seems like yesterday that my great aunt was driving around town in her red convertible with the top down, sunglasses on and wind blowing in her hair . . . or that I was just relocating to New York City to begin an exciting, new career. Now my aunt is in hospice care . . . and I (at the same age she was when she was "tooling down the highway doing 79") am pedaling my bicycle—helmet firmly in place with sunglasses perched on my nose—around another island where I now live.

I'm not quite sure how to slow down and enjoy each moment. Maybe I will begin with just taking each breath . . . a moment at a time.

. . . .

"Yesterday is gone. Tomorrow has not yet come. We have only today. Let us begin."

—Mother Teresa

And Now Our Minds Are One

November is American Indian & Alaska Native Heritage Month. On Thanksgiving Day 2006, I received an email from my dear friend Wilma Mankiller (1945–2010), the first woman to be elected Principal Chief of the Cherokee Nation. She shared with me a Thanksgiving message that is included in an annual ceremony held at Onondaga. "Reading it several times a year," Wilma wrote, "helps keep things in perspective."

I understand that this Thanksgiving Address was heard in its totality, in Seneca and in English, at the 1977 Geneva Conference. There, early one morning, Seneca Chief Corbett Sundown burned tobacco in an open courtyard, bringing the Indian delegations together.

The prayer is a fairly long one. Here are the Closing Words as my own wishes for you, and in memory of my beloved friend Wilma.

. . . .

"We have now arrived at the place where we end our words
Of all the things we have named, it was not our intention to leave
	anything out . . .
If something was forgotten,
we leave it to each individual to send such greetings and thanks in
	their own way.
And now our minds are one."
	—Haudenosaunee Thanksgiving Prayer

Portions of this essay first appeared as "And Now Our Minds Are One," in *Finding God Day By Day* (Cincinnati, OH: Forward Movement, 2010). Used with permission.

One Hundred Words

What happens? Not how or why, but what? What happens that by thirty words exchanged, we know the way . . . without a map or guide? Seeming to fall into step . . . synchronized . . . word for word . . . phrase for phrase . . . instantly . . . instinctively (38).

Appearing to speak in code . . . one starts . . . the other finishes . . . rarely completing the sentence . . . but always completing the thought (57).

Remembering earlier conversations . . . a month ago . . . a year ago . . . yesterday. Bridging the past to the future . . . the present simply a river to cross (80).

What happens? Not how or why . . . but what? Word for word . . . count with me . . . by one hundred words, we're there (100).

What's Next?

For many years I created a list of yearly resolutions. Some of the items never changed: losing the same ten pounds that stubbornly could not be lost, working toward that next promotion, and keeping my bills and paperwork more orderly. It was easy to make the list of pretty much the same items, with few variations. I seemed to know them by heart, in my heart. I would write them down, fold the slip of paper, put it in my Bible for safekeeping, and refer to it from time to time throughout the year.

That is, until one New Year's Eve when I woke up with a start in the middle of the night. There I go again, I thought to myself, limiting God. Anything and everything on my list I should want *now* and be fully and readily prepared to receive, beginning at this moment. I pulled out the slip of paper from my Bible. Grabbing my pen, I scratched out the date for the new year and wrote down instead only one word: NOW.

On that first day of January, I pulled out the list again. Having changed the future to the present, and no longer focused on career goals nor materials things, I began to write down what I believed God desired for me right now, at that moment. Now on my list were recorded my desires and the treasures of the intangible gifts of the spirit that can never be exhausted. These were my soul's sincerest desires, the ones that had been whispered in my heart and planted deep within my soul.

Today, I am no longer working full time; I certainly have no excuse not to exercise daily to stay in shape, and it's hard to think of anything I really need materially. What will be my New Year's resolutions this year?

Portions of this essay first appeared as "Now," in *Finding God Day By Day* (Cincinnati, OH: Forward Movement, 2010). Used with permission.

What's next? I have been asked that question more than once: after I retired from a twenty-four-year corporate career; after I completed a year-long fellowship up at Harvard; after four years at the Jackie Robinson Foundation; and then once I relocated to Savannah. What's next?

This question reminds me of President Josiah Bartlett, played by Martin Sheen, in that political TV drama *The West Wing*. "What's next?" was what President Bartlett often asked after solving or resolving some seemingly impossible conundrum, often at the end of an episode. In episode 2.9, entitled "Galileo," Mallory O'Brien, who in the series was the daughter of White House Chief of Staff Leo McGarry, asked that infernal question "why" (in this instance, go to Mars) to Sam Seaborn, the Deputy White House Communications Director; he so eloquently answered:

> 'Cause it's next. Because we came out of the cave, and we looked over the hill and we saw fire; and we crossed the ocean and we pioneered the west, and we took to the sky. The history of man is hung on a timeline of exploration . . . and this is what's next.

While you and I may not be going to Mars, the "her-story" or the "his-story" of "our-story" is also hung on a timeline of exploration. Whatever is next is what's next. 'Cause it's next.

What's next for you and for me as we approach a new year? Perhaps the answer to this question may be found in a speech delivered at The Lord Mayor's Luncheon at Mansion House on November 10, 1942 (after a victory at "The Battle of Egypt" following a series of defeats from Dunkirk to Singapore), when Winston Churchill stated, "Now this is not the end. It is not even the beginning of the end. But it is, perhaps, the end of the beginning."

Yes, dear friends, you will one day be coming to the end of whatever you are doing right now. And while this may be the end of your beginning of life as it has been . . . or had been . . . it certainly does *not* need to be your end, for together we will continue to explore beyond our horizons.

Just remember, in this drama called "My Life"—for which there is no dress rehearsal—you are only beginning Act II, Scene II. Get ready to go out on the stage and to begin dancing from the inside out. 'Cause it's next.

· · · · · · · · · · · ·

All I want to do right now is dance. Feel the music pulsating in me. Dancing from the inside out. Twirling around, standing my ground. Laughing with glee.

I need to dance more.

—Westina Matthews

ACKNOWLEDGMENTS

Let me begin to thank all of those who have received my weekly reflections over the years and encouraged me to publish a collection in a book; especially Patty Mingledorf, and Mary Kaye Fullenkamp, who have always taken the time to comment on every single reflection. Words fail me to express my deepest gratitude to Anne Mallonee, Tom Milligan, Doris Buchanan Johnson, Pamela Clift, Chee Chee Williams, Robyn Ince, and Carolyn Green for your thoughtful comments on the early drafts. An extra hug to my sister Domina Matthews Page who not only read every reflection, corrected me on some of the family antics, and suggested the title for the book but also has both prayed and laughed along with me as I figure out how to grow old gracefully.

The Church Publishing staff have been wonderful, and working with Nancy Bryan as my editor has been a sheer joy. I am most appreciative of Forward Movement, *Sacred Journey: The Journal of Fellowship in Prayer*, the Episcopal Café, the *University of Dayton Magazine*, and the Erma Bombeck Writers' Workshop for giving me permission to use portions of previously published essays in this book.

I have dedicated this book to my dear, sweet Great Aunt Betsy Berry (who was "Mom" to me for over forty years, and who died at the age of ninety-nine and nine months, just as I was completing this book). Before she became too ill, I would read to her every single reflection that was about either her or the cast of characters in our family. In clearing out her files, I found folders bulging with everything I had ever published or had been written about me. She was my biggest cheerleader and fan.

Dedicated in my heart is my beloved husband Alan Shatteen, who has been so supportive of my living into my call to write, to speak, to teach, and to love; I could not have continued on this journey without him.

Last but far from least, I give honor and glory to God who is the Alpha and the Omega, the beginning and the end, the source of my inspiration, and the balm of my Gilead.